MW01073772

Tendon Nei Kung

Building Strength, Power, and
Flexibility in the Joints

Mantak Chia

Destiny Books
Rochester, Vermont

Destiny Books
One Park Street
Rochester, Vermont 05767
www.DestinyBooks.com

Destiny Books is a division of Inner Traditions International

Originally published in Thailand in 2006 by Universal Tao Publications under the
title *Tendon Nei Kung: Opening and Growing Tendon Power*

Library of Congress Cataloging-in-Publication Data
Chia, Mantak, 1944–
  Tendon nei kung : building strength, power, and flexibility in the joints / Mantak
Chia.
     p. cm.
  "Originally published in Thailand in 2006 by Universal Tao Publications under the
title Tendon Nei Kung : Opening and Growing Tendon Power."
  Includes index.
  ISBN 978-1-59477-187-3 (pbk.)
  1. Qi gong. 2. Hygiene, Taoist. 3. Tendons. I. Title.
  RA781.8.C4695 2009
  613.7'1489—dc22

                                                                                            2009001343

Printed and bound in India by Replika Press Pvt. Ltd.

10 9 8 7 6 5 4 3 2 1

Text design and layout by Jon Desautels
This book was typeset in Janson with Present used as the display typeface

Contents

Acknowledgments

We extend our gratitude to the many generations of Taoist masters who have passed on their special lineage, in the form of an unbroken oral transmission, over thousands of years. We wish to especially thank Taoist Master Yi Eng for his patience and openness in transmitting the formulas of Taoist Inner Alchemy. We also wish to thank the thousands of unknown men and women of the Chinese healing arts who developed many of the methods and ideas presented in this book.

We offer our eternal gratitude to our parents and teachers for their many gifts to us. Remembering them brings joy and satisfaction to our continued efforts in presenting the Universal Tao System. As always, their contribution has been crucial in presenting the concepts and techniques of the Universal Tao.

Thanks to Juan Li for the use of his beautiful and visionary paintings and drawings, illustrating the Taoist esoteric practices.

We thank the many contributors essential to this book's final form: The editorial and production staff at Inner Traditions/Destiny Books for their efforts to clarify the text and produce a handsome new edition of the book and Nancy Ringer for her line edit of the new edition.

We wish to thank the following people for their assistance in producing the previous editions of this book: Pierre Morton for his writing and editorial contributions; Udon for his illustrations, book layout, and cover design; Dennis Huntington and Jean Chilton for their editorial and proofreading assistance; and Jettaya Phaobtong and Saumya Comer for their editorial contributions to the first revised edition of the book.

A special thank you goes to our Thai Production Team: Raruen Keawpadung, Computer Graphics; Saysunee Yongyod, Photographer; Udon Jandee, Illustrator; and Saniem Chaisarn, Production Designer.

Finally, we wish to thank our certified instructors, students, and sponsors throughout the world for their ongoing contributions to the system and for preserving the vitality of the Universal Tao practices.

Putting Tendon Nei Kung into Practice

The practices described in this book have been used successfully for thousands of years by Taoists trained by personal instruction. Readers should not undertake these practices without receiving personal transmission and training from a certified instructor of the Universal Tao, since some of these practices, if done improperly, may cause injury or result in health problems. This book is intended to supplement individual training by the Universal Tao System and to serve as a reference guide for these practices. Anyone who undertakes these practices on the basis of this book alone, does so entirely at his or her own risk.

The meditations, practices, and techniques described herein are not intended to be used as an alternative or substitute for professional medical treatment and care. If any readers are suffering from illnesses based on mental or emotional disorders, an appropriate professional health care practitioner or therapist should be consulted. Such problems should be corrected before training begins.

Neither the Universal Tao nor its staff and instructors can be responsible for the consequences of any practice or misuse of the information contained in this book. If the reader undertakes any exercise without strictly following the instructions, notes, and warnings, the responsibility must lie solely with the reader.

This book does not attempt to give any medical diagnosis, treatment, prescription, or remedial recommendation whatsoever, in relation to any human disease, ailment, suffering, or physical condition.

Words on the Tao

It has been said that the Tao that can be told is not the eternal Tao. This phrase suggests that the Tao (God, universe, life) is so unfathomable that to think we can understand all of this wonderful life is simply an unrealistic notion (fig. 1.1). Besides, is it not the great unknown that keeps us going, that keeps us so fascinated and intrigued with this multifaceted, infinitely fantastic thing we call life? In the West, there

Fig. 1.1. Limitless Tao

is a tendency to try to intellectualize every possible aspect of life and strive to give a logical explanation for it. The truth of the matter is that if we spend all of our time *thinking* about life, we will never move into the *feeling* of it, and we will miss life's greatest vehicle for joy and happiness.

We should not let the realization that there will always be an aspect of mystery in life, that there will always be something that we cannot understand, create any notions of insecurity or fear within us. Rather, we should learn to embrace this mystery and allow its unfathomable greatness to inspire us. In this way, all sacred knowledge will unfold within us in due course (fig. 1.2). We do know that the word *tao* means "the way" or, more to the point, "the natural way." Contrary to what seems to be today's popular belief, Taoists believe that human beings' natural state is to be joyful, healthy, and virtuous. Therefore, in order to lead a fulfilling existence we need only to get and stay in touch with our inner being. In other words, we must be at one with

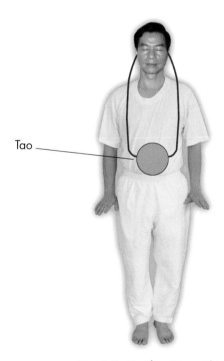

Tao

Fig. 1.2. Limitless Tao within

the Tao. This, of course, is easier said than done. However, it is still a great relief to tap into the powerful truth and simplicity of the Tao. So wherever you go and whatever path you follow, remember the Taoist philosophy: you are inherently "good," made out of pure joy, love, and infinite potential.

BENEFITS OF BEING AWARE OF THE TAO

With today's artificial lifestyle we inevitably encounter experiences that pull and push us out of our primal states of being. From childhood we encounter numerous confusing experiences and are taught a variety of behaviors that contradict our natural and happy state. The results of these experiences are that we are eventually led away from our inner being and ultimately forget how to live without struggle. Running here and there chasing our tails, we forget what it is we really want. Caught up in the vicious circle of cause and effect, we forget who we really are. Many religions supply us with a multitude of rules and regulations in an effort to help stop this cycle, but in many cases they only add more frustration to our lives and contribute to the problem, not the solution.

Being aware of the Tao entails simply quieting our "monkey mind," or intellect, and going inside. The intellect, of course, serves a good purpose, but most present-day cultures place so much emphasis on developing the intellect in early youth that it soon dominates our other thinking or choice-making mechanism—our heart or instinct. When we are in our natural state our choices are always made based on what our heart tells us. The heart is an unfailing choice-making mechanism, but most of us don't recognize its fantastic intelligence, and because of our upbringing we spend our lives referring to our intellect for information about all levels of life. Never taking the time to still our intellect and go inside results in this hyperactive, over-stimulated, and ultimately out-of-control mind that is responsible for much of our unhappiness. The worst part of the problem is that people don't realize what the problem is!

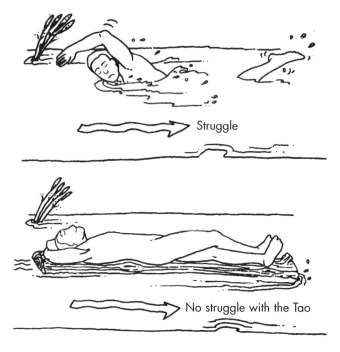

Fig. 1.3. Guidance from our inner Tao

The Universal Tao System provides a number of great techniques, such as, among others, the Inner Smile, to help us regain our "heart-mind." There are also meditations, such as the Microcosmic Orbit, that allow us to reconnect with our internal energy. Using these techniques, we are able to again sense the ebb and flow of life's rather predictable patterns. We can then simply align ourselves with them instead of repeatedly trying to force and struggle our way upstream against the current (fig. 1.3).

THE CAUSE OF ILLNESS ACCORDING TO TAOIST PHILOSOPHY AND CHINESE MEDICINE

The cause of illness, according to Taoist philosophy and Chinese medicine, intimately coincides with the phrase "being aware of the Tao." On a physical level, when we are aware of the Tao and in our

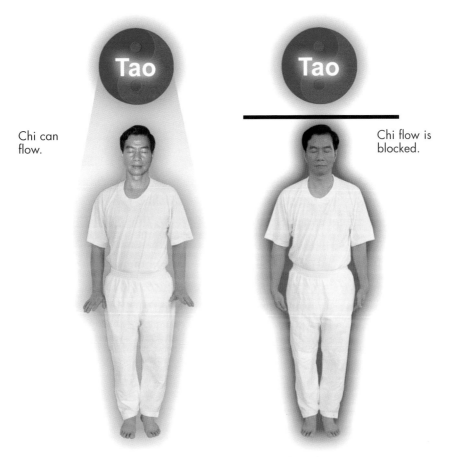

Chi can
flow.

Chi flow is
blocked.

Fig. 1.4. Ignorance of the Tao leads to disease.

natural state our bodies are relaxed and supple. The vital energy, or
chi, is able to flow freely through our energy pathways or meridians.
When this energy is allowed to flow freely, it nourishes our body's
cells, yielding a healthy, strong body and a youthful appearance.
Our immune system becomes strong and we are able to think with
more clarity. On the other hand, when we are ignorant of the Tao we
inevitably run into fear-provoking situations. As the ancient Taoists
discovered, fear causes tension and ultimately causes kinks in our
meridians. The blockages of these meridians are the causes of all illness (dis-ease) (fig. 1.4).

THE KEY TO HEALTH AND HAPPINESS
IS THE TAO

Being in touch with the Tao is vital to leading a healthy and fulfilling life. It has been said that in the pursuit of knowledge every day something is learned, but in the pursuit of the Tao every day something must be dropped. This is not to say that we must throw away all knowledge, but rather that we must make an effort to drop our "personality masks" so that we can get in touch with our natural selves. How do we drop our personality masks? We are faced with two choices: to act in accordance with the Tao (love) or to act out of fear. To cultivate happiness and thus health in our lives, we need to consistently and conscientiously base all of our choices on what is truly natural to us . . . the Tao (fig. 1.5). Choosing from love, we will force ourselves to start stripping away our fear-based personality masks. As a result, we can start living our lives guided by the wisdom within, instead of the chaos without.

Fig. 1.5. Following the Tao leads to happiness.

An Introduction to Tendon Nei Kung

Although regular practice of Tendon Nei Kung may yield a vast number of benefits, the exercise is specifically designed to aid in the growth and strengthening of the tendons. The latest research on the human body reveals that for cultivating strength and physical well-being, the tendons are a vital ingredient. Generally speaking, people have a very limited knowledge about tendons and are far more interested in knowing how to pump and tone their muscles in order to appear strong externally. To cultivate true strength, however, the tendons must be strengthened as well. Before we go into explaining the exercise itself, though, it will be helpful to have some basic knowledge about tendons and their nature.

TENDONS AND LIGAMENTS

Tendons and ligaments are types of connective tissue. Tendons connect bones to muscles (see fig. 2.1 on page 8), while ligaments connect bones to other bones (see fig. 2.2 on page 8). Ligaments are found mainly between joints and are generally short in length. Tendons, on the other hand, are located throughout the body and can be quite long. For example, the Achilles tendon, which connects our heel bone

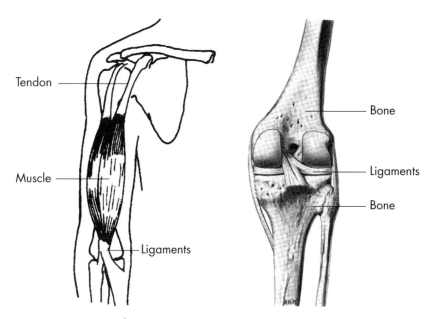

Tendon

Muscle

Ligaments

Bone

Ligaments

Bone

Fig. 2.1. Tendons connect
bones to muscles.

Fig. 2.2. Ligaments connect
bones to other bones.

to our calf muscle, is of prominent length. Throughout this book we will refer mostly to tendons. However, the Tendon Nei Kung practices are as beneficial to ligaments as they are to tendons. Bear in mind that when we say "tendons" we are referring to the body's connective tissues in general and are hence referring to the ligaments as well.

GENERAL CHARACTERISTICS
Tendons Recycle Energy

Tendons can be thought of as extremely strong rubber bands, especially when they are intelligently developed. Their elastic nature allows them to absorb energy, stretch, and whip back, returning 93 percent of the energy they absorbed. If you have developed your tendons and have the know-how, you can use them to recycle energy with very little loss of power (fig. 2.3).

Fig. 2.3. Engaged
tendon ready to
recycle energy

Tendon Power Is Long Lasting

Underdeveloped tendons require consistent practice over an extended period of time to yield significant results. One of their main attributes, however, is that once they have been intelligently and sufficiently strengthened, they maintain their cultivated strength. If we lead a relatively healthy lifestyle, practice of Tendon Nei Kung will yield a substantial strength that will serve us even into the last years of our lives. Muscle power, on the other hand, can be built up in a matter of days, but muscles are apt to lose their power in a very short time if they are not continually stimulated.

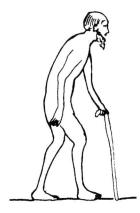

Fig. 2.4. A feeble body has become the norm for elderly people.

Muscles also require harsh exercise to maintain their strength. Generally speaking, while we are still youthful building up our muscles is not difficult and is usually a natural result of our active lifestyle. As we move into old age, though, exercising the muscles becomes ever more inconvenient, for both physical reasons and lack of free time. It is not hard to find proof for the harshness of this reality; simply by looking at elderly people today, we can see how tragically feeble they have become, having to strain themselves to do the most basic of physical activities such as jogging or even walking (fig. 2.4). Even the best of our ex-athletes grow old and weak despite their attempts to keep their physical bodies strong with muscle-building exercises. This enfeeblement has accompanied aging for so long that it has been accepted as the norm, and even as a natural process. This is not how it has to be, though. If people had just a little more knowledge about their physical and energetic bodies, they could spare themselves much physical suffering.

Tendons Are Durable

Besides being able to maintain their strength over a life span, tendons also take a lot longer than muscles to tire while engaged in physical activity. To illustrate this point, see how long you can hang on a bar with your arms bent, making use of your biceps muscles to hold you up (fig. 2.5).

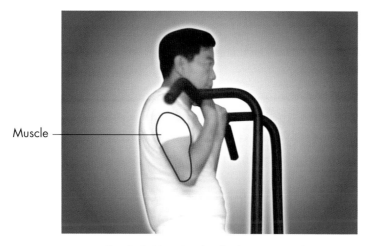

Muscle

Fig. 2.5. Hanging by the biceps muscles

Then attempt the same feat but keep your arms straight, locking the joints but keeping the muscles as relaxed as possible, in this way making use of your tendons to suspend your body (fig. 2.6). Unless you possess a superhuman strength you will invariably find it a lot more challenging to hold on to the bar when you are using your muscles as your primary support.

Fig 2.6. Hanging by the arm tendons

Tendons Can Store Chi

In Tai Chi Chi Kung practice it is a well-known fact that the tendons are the secret to manifesting great power. Besides their inherent elasticity and strength, tendons also have the fantastic ability to channel and store chi. One of the main areas where chi is stored in the tendons (and ligaments) is the joints (fig. 2.7). For this reason, the practice of Tendon Nei Kung greatly aids in preventing and curing arthritis, as the poisonous uric acid that causes arthritic conditions is forced out of the body to make space for the healing energy we call chi.

Tendon Nei Kung's detoxifying qualities makes drinking sufficient amounts of water extremely important, especially when you are attempting the practice for the first time. If you start packing and storing chi in your joints, forcing out the uric acid, and you do not have enough water in your system to flush this acid, it may stagnate in your body, making you temporarily ill.

Chi storage

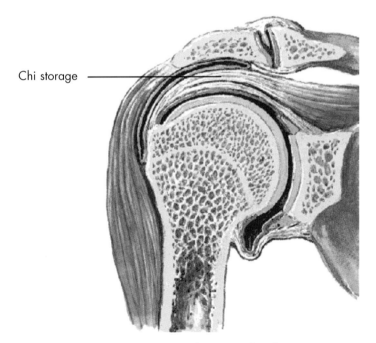

Fig. 2.7. Chi is stored in the joints.

Strengthening Tendons Can Prevent Injury

Damaging a tendon in any way is usually a severe injury (fig. 2.8). It is common knowledge among athletes that it is far better to break a bone than to damage a tendon. As anyone who has done so before will tell you, injuring a tendon is an extremely painful experience. More than that, tendons heal a lot more slowly than injuries to muscles or bones, and depending on the tendon that is injured, such an injury can be very debilitating. In extreme cases, some tendon injuries never

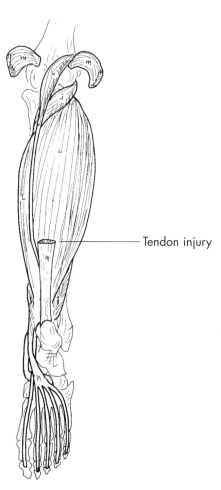

Tendon injury

Fig. 2.8. A weak tendon is
vulnerable to injury.

heal to full strength. By using the Taoist practices one can heal injured tendons with great success over a period of time. Nevertheless, it is far better to strengthen tendons before they get injured instead of trying to repair them afterward.

Tendons Unite the Body

As previously mentioned, tendons connect our bones to muscles and ligaments connect bones to bones. Having strong muscles and bones is useful for physical activity, but if our tendons are underdeveloped, then our movements will be disconnected, making controlled, balanced movement almost impossible to achieve. The more we develop our tendons, the more we unite and connect our body and allow our various body parts to function as a unit.

After joining a decent Tai Chi or Yoga class, people often report that they feel more connected and coordinated in their movement. They don't realize how accurate their statement is. The natural workout yielded by Tai Chi and Yoga strengthens the tendons, and practitioners literally become more tightly knit.

When the tendons and muscles are nurtured and built up together, they eventually form one big solid piece of fascia rising from the toes to the top of the neck. This unification of the body greatly aids fluidity in movement. Almost all legendary athletes, no matter which field, have been noted to have a more fluid style of executing their specific discipline. Even in a rigid sport such as boxing, for example, Muhammad Ali was able to express fantastic fluidity, grace, and style; he is said to be the best boxer of all time and is also famous for his statement, "Float like a butterfly, sting like a bee." A brief look at nature also reveals that even the mightiest of beasts is not without fluidity and balance in movement. Yet these qualities are a rarity among our everyday athletes, especially those who take part in contact sports. Most of their time is unfortunately spent dully building up their muscles in the hope of achieving athletic superiority.

Tendon Power

Tendons have the ability to absorb energy, stretch like elastic, and release up to 93 percent of the energy they absorb. This is the reason a superior long-distance runner's strides seem so effortless. Good long-distance runners, whether consciously or unconsciously, have worked out how to allow their tendons, rather than their muscles, to do most of the work.

The big tendon at the back of a long-distance runner's leg, the Achilles tendon, extends and absorbs the force from the impact of the leg supporting the body during a stride (fig. 3.1). When it reaches its maximum capacity the tendon contracts, giving back 93 percent of

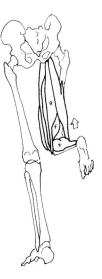

Fig. 3.1. A long-distance runner's engaged Achilles tendon

the force with which the runner's foot made impact with the ground, just like an elastic band or spring. This tendon recoil greatly assists in propelling the runner forward. With the 7 percent assistance provided by the muscles as extra momentum, the runner can maintain his or her running speed for extended distances with ease, being highly economical with his or her energy.

The elasticity of tendons is a prominent part of the secret to the power of the Tai Chi Chi Kung position Ward Off (all yang energy). When an opponent pushes on the Ward Off arm of a well-practiced Tai Chi Chi Kung practitioner who knows how to align, lock the structure, root, and relax his or her muscles, the large tendons in the back of the practitioner's leg, lower back, and shoulder are allowed to stretch and absorb the force (fig. 3.2). At the will of the practitioner, 93 percent of the force that is now stored in the tendons can be released back into the opponent. The Tai Chi Chi Kung practitioner can then add his or her own force with his or her legs, lumbar spine, and hips, not to mention the possibility of internal force. The result is that the opponent, regardless of size, will be overwhelmed with strength and repelled some distance.

Although Tai Chi Chi Kung practitioners have this option in a martial situation, it is usually seen as more intelligent and effective to yield to force than to meet it head-on, as in Roll Back (all yin energy).

Fig. 3.2. In Tai Chi, tendon strength is used to absorb and reflect force.

THE WESTERN CONCEPT OF ATHLETICISM VS. THE ANCIENT TAOISTS' UNDERSTANDING

Chi Follows Yi (Energy Follows Mind)

An old Tai Chi saying goes, "If you want to create something worthwhile, you have to use the mind a little." This is the underlying difference between Western and esoteric exercise. Generally speaking, in the West there is a consensus that you use your mind when busy with "desk work" or academics, but when you take the time to improve your physical condition, you may leave your mind free to drift wherever it would like to go. There is a very good reason that Taoists are so concerned with harnessing the mind while exercising the physical body: they long ago discovered what today's scientists are rediscovering—energy can be led with the mind. When this meditation in motion takes place, physical capabilities are increased many times. Many Western athletes have experienced this meditation in motion, or what they term "being in the zone." For example, it is common for long-distance runners to become so concentrated in their pursuit that they lose track of time completely. Once athletes have experienced this state of absorption or meditation, they recognize how valuable it is to their performance. In effect, their will for achievement was so great that it helped their mind to become very concentrated. The concentrated mind could then help direct more chi to the relevant muscles and tendons, greatly increasing their performance. Unfortunately, most athletes who have experienced this state don't know how they got there or how to how to get back into it.

Muscles

Since ancient Greece, Western society has been developing an ever more narrow scope concerning the subject of how to develop the human body so that it may be strong and healthy. Athletic games were a huge part of ancient Greek culture, and as a result most young men turned their attention to becoming athletes so that they could have the respect of their society. For most of the young men of that time it was most important to look the part of an athlete, even if they did not compete as athletes, in order to be respected. Because of this fanaticism, outer-body sculpting soon became the hobby of most of the young men, all trying to look like the perfect athlete.

Even today, when Westerners think of a superior athlete they usually think of big, bulky, bulging muscles. Muscles are what we can see, and so for the most part people concentrate solely on them. Seeing a muscular figure, subconsciously we perceive that figure to possess a primitive power and to be more attractive. In many cases women are more sexually aroused by a muscular build than by a weak, thin, or flabby-looking body. It is undoubtedly true that muscles yield a portion of strength and that they are a necessary component of a healthy, athletic body. However, ancient Tai Chi Chi Kung, some sects of advanced Kung Fu, and Yoga practitioners have long since had a viewpoint different from that of the general Western conception of athleticism and strength. One of the main points of difference is that in their view, the ideal muscle is not rock hard and bulky, as the Western world favors, but rather (when relaxed) soft and supple, allowing chi to flow through the body. When it's time for action, though, and the muscles are engaged, then they become extremely hard. The difference is that the muscles are both hard and soft (yin and yang) and not in a constant state of tension, blocking the flow of energy.

These advanced concepts of the human body were derived simply by looking at nature. For instance, when we look at the mighty tiger we can easily see that although this beast obviously possesses extreme power and strength, its muscles seem totally relaxed when not engaged (fig. 3.3). We can also see that there is not one muscle that is overly developed compared to the next but rather that they are in natural proportion to one another, allowing the body components to work together as a unit.

Fig. 3.3. A tiger's muscles are supple and relaxed when not engaged. Each is in natural proportion to the rest, allowing the tiger's body to function smoothly and gracefully, with a free flow of chi.

Tendons

Another point of difference between Western and Taoist perceptions of athleticism is that Western athletes lack awareness of their tendons (not to mention their organs and chi) and the tendons' wonderful potential when intelligently developed. Looking at nature, Taoists observed that many of the more fleet-footed and powerful animals had not big, muscular legs but rather thin, almost completely tendon-occupied legs. Two examples of this phenomenon are the antelope and the horse. The antelope is an obviously nimble creature that walks and runs great distances every day in impressive time, often over very challenging terrain. The horse is known to be both a graceful and a powerful runner and can easily clear great heights if need be. Yet in both these skilled runners we see that the legs are noticeably smaller in proportion to the rest of the body. Upon closer examination we find that their legs have almost no muscle on them at all.

Fig. 3.4. Thanks to the well-developed tendons in its legs, the antelope has amazing speed and jumping ability.

Fig. 3.5. Like the antelope, the horse has much more tendon than muscle in its legs, giving it great speed and power.

Instead, they consist of bones and a lot of well-developed tendons. This is the secret to the antelope and horse's fantastic running and jumping abilities (figs. 3.4 and 3.5).

Unfortunately, today's style of training the body concerns repeatedly lifting weights with movements that engage only individual muscles. The tendons remain undeveloped and weak, as do the smaller, nonvisible muscles. This leaves the tendons more vulnerable to injury; it's the reason why many of today's sports stars have apparently well-toned bodies but often end up with long-term tendon injuries. When a tendon is snapped or torn it takes an exceedingly long time to heal. In fact, a broken bone will heal considerably faster than a torn tendon. These underdeveloped tendons are put to extensive use by athletes and inevitably take strain. The problems usually manifest in the vital joints, such as the knees, where there are many tendons. An athlete may be able to overcome such an injury for a time, but it usually ends up being a nagging, recurring problem that heavily upsets the momentum of an athlete's career, if it does not stop it in its tracks for good.

One of the ancient Taoists' secrets to being able to wield amazing strength even at a very advanced age was their awareness and knowledge of their tendons. (Of course, tendons weren't all that they studied, as they realized the importance of nurturing the body as a whole—mind, body, and soul.) They spent many years studying nature and developing exercises that would strengthen their tendons in the best possible way (fig. 3.6). The results of their efforts were stupendous,

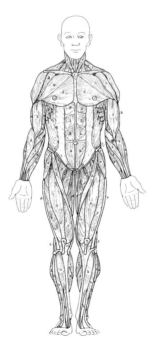

Fig. 3.6. Well-developed tendons are the secret to true physical strength.

Fig. 3.7. When mind, body, and spirit work together, even an old man can exert considerable force.

allowing them to achieve skills in the martial arts and a state of physical well-being that to today's man seem almost unbelievable.

When an old man of slight build can push a heavily built figure a distance of 30 yards or more, people gasp and say that it is superhuman. Actually it is simply the result of what can be achieved when mind, body, and spirit are intelligently developed and are allowed to work as a unit. Everybody has this potential. Of course the Tao does not approve of or encourage violence. The illustration of the old man wielding a fantastic strength is simply one of the grosser manifestations of following the Tao and is used only because it is tangible and easily understood example. It is only an indication of the potential that can be derived when a human being is developed as a whole, all of the mind, all of the body, and all of the spirit (fig. 3.7).

TAOIST PRACTICES FOR TODAY'S ATHLETES

A very obvious example of the potential of tendons are the experiences of Universal Tao Senior Instructor Peter Kontaxak. Peter used to be part of the Greek athletics team and held the Greek record for the long jump. During his competitive days, Peter had to bring his promising career to a sudden halt when he started experiencing pain in his knee and soon even lost the ability to run. Doctors told him he had "jumper's leg" and would have to go through a risky knee operation if he wished to continue with his career.

Peter was not prepared to take this risk, however. He was well aware of the implications and risks of such an operation from his fellow athletes. Many people who undergo such operations come out unable to compete anyway. Even those who do receive benefit often find that the restoration of their knee is only temporary, and they find themselves with the same problem later in their career.

Peter began research on alternative options and soon came across the methods of the Universal Tao System. He immediately started applying the practices that were shown to him at the Tao Garden. He studied and practiced the Inner Smile and the Microcosmic Orbit meditations to increase his sensitivity to his body and increase his chi flow, giving him a good base for self-healing. He proceeded to work on healing on his knee, making use of healing methods such as Chi Massage and Mung Bean Hitting (see chapter 8). Once he felt the tendons in his knee had sufficiently healed, Peter continued with Taoist strengthening exercises, gradually increasing the time he spent with Embracing the Tree or Iron Shirt Chi Kung. On the recommendation of the Tao Garden, Peter also made good use of hanging exercises, which he claimed helped him tremendously with his strength. (The hanging exercise is done by hanging from a bar so that one's feet are on the ground. This practice should be built up slowly so as not to stress any tendons, but eventually one should practice by hanging from a bar for four sets of at least 40 seconds. The hands can be alternated between being held straight above the shoulders and being held at a wider angle. Eventually one may also attempt one-handed hanging.)

Peter tells how the strength that he attained from traditional weight-lifting exercises greatly differed from the feeling of strength that he achieved from using the Taoist strengthening exercises. He says that the weight training undoubtedly made him feel more powerful but that he somehow felt that power to be external. The Taoist practices, he says, yielded a different feeling of strength, one that seemed to grow from the inside out. This strength seemed to include all of his body, rather than coming from specific isolated muscles, such as his thigh muscles, triceps, or biceps. This gave him the feeling of being very compact, nimble, and strong. Peter's tale correlates well with the ideology of Taoist and Yogic exercises, which claim to strengthen the body from the inside out, greatly uniting it by developing all the nonvisible smaller muscles and of course tendons, yielding a strength much different from that of someone who concentrates solely on his obvious muscles.

Peter goes on to describe many astounding experiences he had when he returned to train and compete with his team. One event that left him as surprised as anyone else was when he discovered that he could now lift an additional thirty kilograms in one of his weight-lifting exercises—this after he had done only the hanging and Embracing the Tree training, without touching a weight during that time. He says that in the past, even when he had done specific weight-training programs with protein diets, the best he could have improved in such an exercise over a similar period of time was by 10 kilograms. Peter's first return to the long jump was also a pleasant surprise, for he came astonishingly close to beating his prior record, and this was without being at his peak fitness level.

Besides the obvious benefits Peter received from these practices, he claims that the most important skill he gained was knowledge of how to concentrate his mind and chi in preparation for a competition and, most importantly, how to "listen" to his organs. This sensitivity gave him the invaluable ability to sense when something was wrong in his body before it actually surfaced. If something was not right, he could get whatever help was necessary before it seriously affected him. This allowed him to maintain his health over his career.

Benefits for Everyday People

The importance of having strong tendons is by no means limited to aspiring athletes. Indeed, it is vital to anyone who wishes to live a truly healthy, happy life.

Tendon strength is durable and long lasting. Tendons, unlike muscles, can provide considerable physical strength even for people well into their old age. Having strong tendons radically lowers one's chances of suffering the indignity of not being able to enjoy basic physical activities.

Tendon Nei Kung and Iron Shirt practice is also vital for spiritual development. Many people hastily want to connect with the "Source" without properly preparing their body. Tendon Nei Kung and Iron Shirt practice makes the tendons supple and strong while also opening up the joints. Raw energy can then be stored in these open spaces in the joints and between the tendons, allowing us to take in more energy. Once this is done, we can start to transform this raw energy into higher creative and spiritual energy.

Practicing the Tendon Nei Kung forms is fantastic exercise for the all-important spinal cord. Recent research has confirmed the ancient Taoist theory that there is a direct relationship between specific sections of the spinal cord and the organs. Tendon Nei Kung thus benefits our organs, too, which are vital to our health.

Chi pressure is also developed by this practice. Chi pressure protects the organs from external damage, just as the air in a tire protects the rim of a wheel (fig. 3.8). People who have a well-developed Iron Shirt and Tendon Nei Kung practice usually gain the ability to take

Fig. 3.8. Air pressure protects the rim of a wheel.

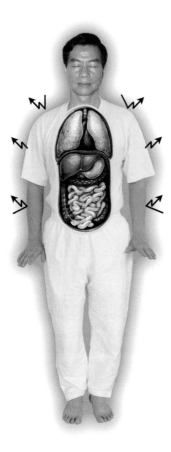

Fig 3.9. Chi pressure protects the internal organs.

a major kick or punch in the abdominal area without any pain or injury to their vital organs (fig. 3.9). (However, once such an ability has been cultivated, Taoist practitioners do not see fit to boast by showing it off.)

REQUIRED PRACTICES THAT SUPPORT TENDON NEI KUNG

To receive the proper benefits of Tendon Nei Kung, you must have a background practice. The standing meditation Iron Shirt Chi Kung is an essential ingredient, as it assists the practitioner in cultivating relaxation, aligning the spine, rooting, strengthening the tendons, and opening the joints. The Inner Smile and Microcosmic Orbit meditations are also vital. Together they will help us increase our chi and then learn how to direct it to where it is needed.

Practicing the Iron Shirt Chi Kung Stance

Your practice of Iron Shirt Chi Kung is vital! Iron Shirt practice is responsible for helping you to cultivate the proper structure and alignment for Tendon Nei Kung. The stance taken up for doing the Tendon Nei Kung forms is exactly the same as for Iron Shirt Chi Kung (fig. 3.10).

1. Stand with your feet in a line, more or less parallel. The correct distance for the feet to be apart is the length of the lower leg from the knees to the toes.
2. Bend your knees slightly, without extending them over your toes, and twist them outward, as if you were pushing against a force pushing inward.
3. Keep your sacrum slightly tucked and your lumbar spine pushed out, correcting the S curve in your back and sending the weight of your upper body to your feet.

Fig. 3.10. The Iron Shirt Chi Kung stance

4. Keep your shoulders and chest as relaxed as possible. Let your chest sink in slightly, helping more upper-body weight drop to your legs.
5. Hold your head as if the crown were suspended by a string from the heavens, while keeping your neck as relaxed and soft as possible.
6. Hold your arms out in front of your body at about shoulder height, as though you were embracing a big tree, while keeping your elbows and shoulders down and completely relaxed.

Adhering to these guidelines should bring your back into proper alignment and help you be in the correct posture to attempt adding the rhythmical movement of the Tendon Nei Kung forms.

The Inner Smile

With the advent of the new millennium, the Cosmic Inner Smile serves as a more powerful beginning practice for new students and experienced practitioners alike. It helps us learn to connect the positive virtue energy of the vital organs with corresponding universal energy by using the simple smile that we learned as a baby (fig. 3.11). This has the effect of increasing our positive power for health, happiness, and spiritual evolution.

1. Sit on the edge of a chair with your hands held together and eyes closed.
2. Re-create a happy emotional state, and express it with your best smile. Smile with your eyes as well, lifting the outer corners of your eyelids, to enhance the process.
3. Picture a radiant smile of energy on the face of a glowing sun directly in front of you.
4. Sense a coolness in your eyes to attract and absorb the warm energy.
5. Mentally enhance the radiance and any color or perceptions of warmth, until your eyes are filled with it.

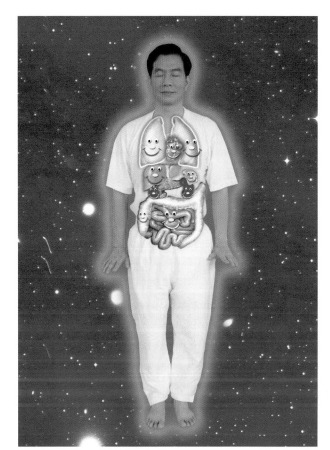

Fig. 3.11. The Inner
Smile

6. Let the smiling energy spread down to your heart, lungs, liver, spleen, and kidneys as you smile to each organ. It is your smile that will give the energy its positive charge.

7. Draw in more energy through your mid-eyebrow and eyes to stimulate the entire system.

The process can take up to 15 minutes before you are ready to circulate the energy in the Microcosmic Orbit.

Opening the Microcosmic Orbit

Opening the Microcosmic Orbit inside you is one of the cornerstones of your Universal Tao practice. An open Microcosmic Orbit enables you to circulate chi (life force) through your body and to expand outward to connect with the forces of nature, the six directions of universal energy, and earth power. Through unique relaxation and concentration techniques, this practice awakens, circulates, directs, and preserves the generative life force, or chi, through the first two major acupuncture channels (or meridians) of the body: the Conception Vessel, which runs down the chest, and the Governing Vessel, which ascends the middle of the back (fig. 3.12). It also teaches us to activate the three internal fires and open the three tan tiens.

1. After completing the Inner Smile, collect the energy at the navel.
2. Let the energy flow down to the sexual center.
3. Move the energy from the sexual center to the perineum.
4. Draw the energy up from the perineum to the sacrum.
5. Draw the energy up to the Ming Men, opposite the navel.

Fig. 3.12. The Microcosmic Orbit

6. Draw the energy up to the eleventh thoracic vertebra (T11).
7. Draw the energy up to the base of the skull.
8. Draw the energy up to the crown and circulate it.
9. Move the energy down from the crown to the mid-eyebrow.
10. Pass the energy down through the tongue to the throat center.
11. Bring the energy down from the throat to the heart center.
12. Bring the energy down to the solar plexus.
13. Bring the energy back to the navel.
14. Circulate the energy through this entire sequence at least 9 or 10 times.
15. Collect the energy at the navel.

Men: Cover your navel with both palms, left hand over right. Collect and mentally spiral the energy at the navel outward 36 times clockwise, and then inward 24 times counterclockwise.

Women: Do the same, only place the right hand over the left and begin by spiraling the energy out from the navel in a counterclockwise direction, then spiral it back to the navel in a clockwise direction.

THE IMPORTANCE OF PRACTICE

We all have mind, body, chi, spirit, nerves, and tendons. If we are given the correct initial guidance, there are no limits to what we can achieve physically, emotionally, and spiritually. Once we have the guidance and we realize that we have all the necessary physical and metaphysical ingredients, we have finally arrived at the beginning of the great path to health and happiness. Once we are at the foot of this path we have already come a long way, and all that we still need is consistent practice. So many people spend their whole life looking outside of themselves for something that they intuitively feel is missing in their lives—some are even encouraged to do so by certain spiritual teachers. The truth is, though, that all the potential and love we need has been within us all this time, just waiting to be explored!

Tendon Nei Kung Practice

The three key instruments that Tendon Nei Kung ("tendon changing") uses to develop the tendons are the mind, heart, and eyes. As a group the mind, heart, and eyes are known in the Chinese language as Yi, which translates as "awareness." The heart is at the very base of this practice. The ancient Taoists followed the theory that the tendons are directly connected to the heart (fig. 4.1). When the heart contracts, the tendons lightly contract. When the heart expands, the tendons expand. Therefore a vital step in Tendon Nei Kung practice is to be able to strongly sense the beating of the heart so that we can move to its rhythm when doing the forms. This is not such a simple task, especially during movement, and it takes a little perseverance. Meditation (the Inner Smile and Microcosmic Orbit) is key. By quieting the mind, we are able to sense the internal organs and really listen to the rhythm of the heart. If you do not have a deep meditation practice and cannot yet feel the contraction and expansion of your heart, it helps to feel your wrist pulse for a moment to get a feel for the rhythm of your heartbeat. (We'll discuss this in more detail in chapter 5.)

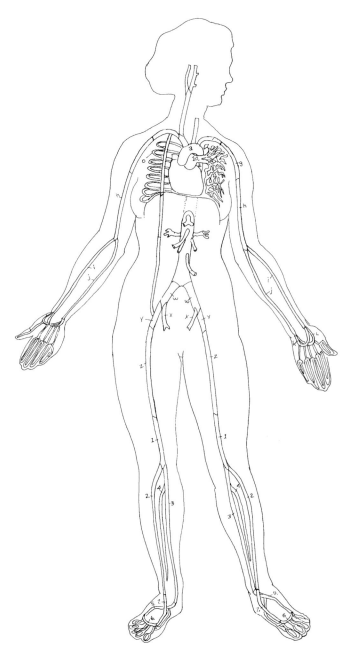

Fig. 4.1. The heart controls the tendons.

THE DIFFERENT FORMS OF CHI

Chi is our life force, our internal energy. Chi is also the energy that permeates the universe. It manifests in an infinite number of ways in our environment. In Tai Chi Chi Kung, however, we deal only with the manifestations that affect our physical, mental, and spiritual well-being. Jing chi, which has come to be known as our original essence, is our sexual energy, and the ancient Taoists believed that we have only a limited amount of it (fig. 4.2). They believed that when this chi is depleted, so are we. Therefore, conservation of this original essence is of primary importance. The Taoists' practice of retaining semen during intercourse is a clear indication of the importance that they give to keeping this sexual energy in the body.

The other two forms of energy that human beings may consume and use are earth chi and heavenly chi. Gross manifestations of these energies are food, water, and the air we breath (all coming from either

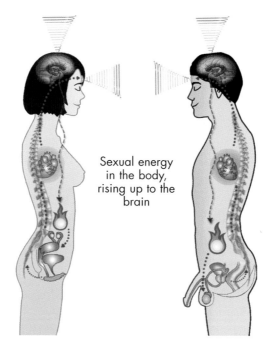

Sexual energy
in the body,
rising up to the
brain

Fig. 4.2. Sexual energy is considered to be the
original force that sustains us.

Fig. 4.3. Earth chi and heavenly chi combine to sustain
human life.

the heavens or the earth). These vital forms of energy (at this stage of our evolution, at least) are simply the manifestations of earth chi and heavenly chi combining and changing into a form that animals and humans can absorb to sustain life (fig. 4.3).

Using the proper techniques, humans are also able to tap into these two great sources of energy directly. This is the basic underlying objective of Tai Chi Chi Kung and many other esoteric practices. In extreme cases, dedicated Yogis and Taoists have achieved states where they no longer need to consume food because they are tapped into a continuous source of heaven and earth energy through their head and feet. Many of the well-known prophets from various religions are believed to have achieved this state in accordance with their enlightenment.

In the Tendon Nei Kung forms we will be dealing specifically with bringing up earth chi, making use of our awareness and certain physical movements to encourage the earth's force to rise up through our bodies, nourishing our tendons (fig. 4.4).

Previous experience with a standing-still practice such as Iron Shirt Chi Kung will greatly assist you in cultivating the ability to move the earth's energy through your feet, legs, and body before routing it out again. If you do not have experience of such a practice, it is highly recommended that you take some time to study this form of Chi Kung. For more detail Master Chia's *Iron Shirt Chi Kung* (Rochester, Vt.: Destiny Books, 2006) comes highly recommended.

Fig. 4.4. Tendon Nei Kung forms draw earth force upward,
nourishing our tendons.

Tendon Nei Kung Forms

 ## Building the Structure for Tendon Nei Kung

The basic movement for the Tendon Nei Kung forms proceeds from the Iron Shirt Chi Kung stance. Once you are in this stance, following the guidelines and principles of relaxation and alignment described earlier, you are ready to begin the movement.

Regardless of style, a universal principle of Tai Chi Chi Kung is that power is generated from below. In other words, when you generate force, it comes from the earth to the feet, up through the legs, up the spine and back, and through the arms, where it will finally be expressed in the hands and fingers (see fig. 5.1 on page 38). Tendon Nei Kung is no different in this regard. In fact, it is the very practice of learning to bring the earth's energy up through your body. The aim is to use the mind, assisted by the correct movements, to bring the earth's energy from the ground through the various tendons of the body and finally into the tendons of the hands.

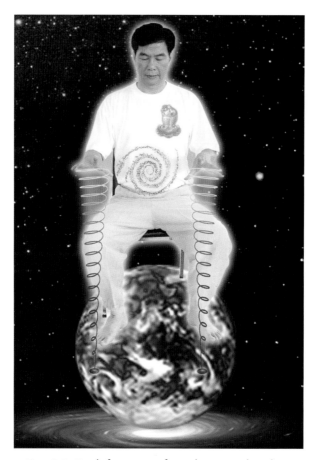

Fig. 5.1. Earth force rises from the ground and up
through the body.

❂ The Feet

Once you have adopted the Iron Shirt stance, you are ready to initiate
the movement from below, or in other words, from the feet. The first
movement involves rocking on your feet.

1. Lift and pull your toes back while gently leaning forward, so that
   your heels rise off the ground about 1 to 1½ inches (fig. 5.2).
2. On return, keep your toes on the ground.

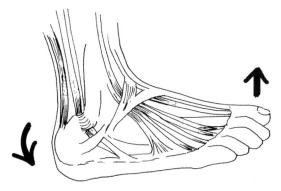

Fig. 5.2. Lifting the toes

❂ The Legs

As you rock forward onto your toes, squeeze your legs slowly from the bottom up (fig. 5.3). The combination of these feet and leg movements should have you moving up and down about 4 to 6 inches. This movement initiates the gentle whipping motion that is used to assist the energy in flowing up to the hand tendons.

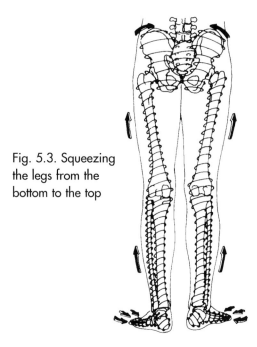

Fig. 5.3. Squeezing the legs from the bottom to the top

❀ The Hips

Once the force has moved from the legs to the hips, press and squeeze the hip joints and feel that the hips are folding on each other (fig. 5.4). Doing this should assist in sending the earth's force upward toward the tendons in the fingers.

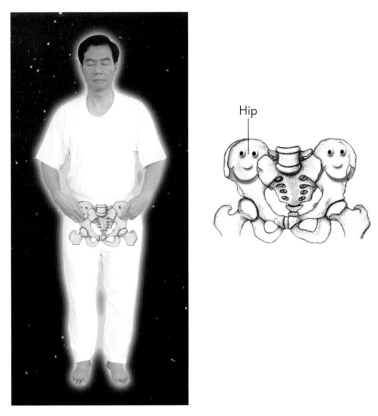

Fig. 5.4. Squeezing the hip joints

The psoas muscle complex is an area of broad, flat muscle in the lower back (fig. 5.5). Like an octopus, it has branches extending out from both sides of the lower spinal vertebrae in many directions. It has two segments at its origin, psoas major and psoas minor, which connect with the twelfth thoracic vertebra (T12) and each of the five lumbar vertebrae (L1 to L5). The psoas major is by far the much larger of the two segments, and it gets most of the attention. The psoas major originates from the transverse processes of T12 and L1 to L5 and passes beneath the inguinal ligament in the groin area as it descends down the front surface of the ilium bones of the pelvis. It inserts into the lesser trochanter process on the inside front of the upper femur bone (the big bone in the upper leg). The smaller psoas minor shares the same origins as the psoas major but inserts into the sacroischial ligament. This ligament connects to the ischium tuberosity (at the back of the pelvis).

Press the psoas muscles from the hip up into the solar plexus and T11. This will help torque the psoas muscles, strongly connecting the hip girth to the leg bone. This connection between the upper and lower body makes the transferral of energy from the ground up far more effective, while also activating the sacral pump. When you are practicing this motion correctly, you will experience the feeling of being very well grounded.

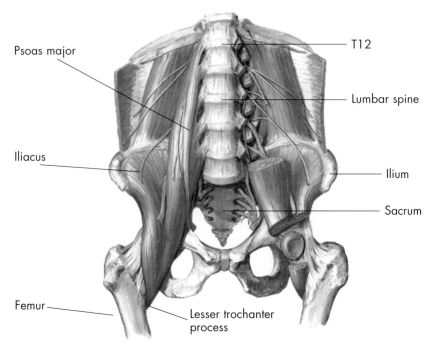

Psoas major

T12

Lumbar spine

Iliacus

Ilium

Sacrum

Femur

Lesser trochanter process

Fig. 5.5. Psoas muscles

� *The Spine*

Feel the momentum of these movements carry into the spine, pushing the energy further up.

1. Stretch the spine upward with a wavelike motion, moving from the bottom up, expanding vertabrae to vertebrae from the five lumbars to the twelve thoracics to the seven cervicals.
2. Lengthen the spine as much as possible without being too forceful, as though someone were slowly pulling an imaginary string suspended from your crown up and slightly forward (fig. 5.6).
3. Really stretch your spine and feel the vital space between the vertebrae opening up and increasing in length, allowing more chi to flow and be stored.

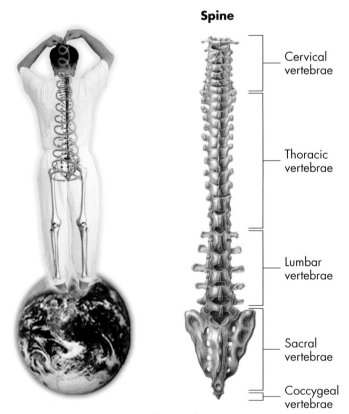

Spine

Cervical vertebrae

Thoracic vertebrae

Lumbar vertebrae

Sacral vertebrae

Coccygeal vertebrae

Fig. 5.6. Lengthening the spine

❂ *The Scapulae*

Open the scapulae and push the T11 vertebra back, simultaneously tilting the sacrum in by rolling your hips under your body (fig. 5.7). You should feel your feet press to the ground as more weight is given to your legs. The movement of the scapulae will give the illusion that your arms are moving forward and back. Take note, however, that your arms are moving not of themselves but only as a consequence of being connected to the scapulae! This is what is referred to as movement without movement in the Taoist texts.

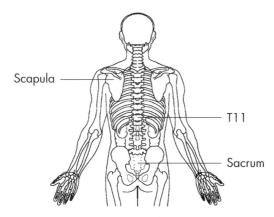

Fig. 5.7. Opening the scapulae

❂ *The Hands*

There is a direct connection between the middle of the hands and the heart. For this reason it is important to gently contract the hands as the heart contracts. By doing so you assist in further synchronizing the beating of the heart with the movement of the tendons. This in turn greatly assists in pulsing more blood and chi through the tendons to the tips of the fingers. As you exhale and torque the various areas of the body and tendons, gently expand your fingers, slightly stretching the finger tendons. Take note that this is a very subtle movement and is not an obvious stretching out of the fingers. Instead, try to sense the blood pulsing into your fingers, moving them as a natural reaction

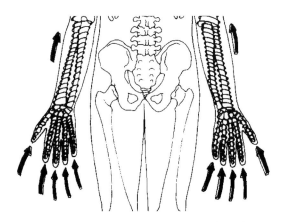

Fig. 5.8. Feel your heartbeat in your hands as
the movement of blood pulsing into your fingers.

to the momentum of the blood repeatedly pouring into them. You
can slightly animate this movement, but do not make the movement
unnatural and unrelated to the heartbeat. Try to sense the blood pulsing in your hands enough to feel as though you actually have a heart in
your hands, and then make your hand movements as a natural reaction
to this pulsing (fig. 5.8).

❂ The Tongue

1. Press your tongue to your palate, connecting the Governing Vessel to the Conception Vessel to close the Microcosmic Orbit and
   activate the cranial pump (fig. 5.9).
2. Now round your shoulders, sink your chest, and push in your chin
   to further open the scapulae and expand your back. This movement will also bring the C7 vertebra into alignment, which will
   send the earth force through the tendons of the arms, the elbows,
   and finally the fingers.
3. As the earth's force reaches your fingers, open your hands to very
   gently stretch the tendons in your fingers. It is vital that you open
   your hands in accordance with the peristaltic pulse you feel in your
   palms.

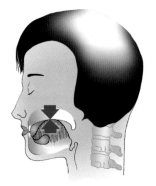

Press your tongue to your palate.

Fig. 5.9. Activating the cranial pump

🌀 The Breath (Chi Pressure)

1. As your heart contracts and you open your hands as explained above, exhale with force by squeezing the tan tien in the lower abdomen, as though you were clenching a fist. This will pull tendons inward toward the tan tien, stretching them (fig. 5.10).

Fig. 5.10. Clenching the tan tien pulls the tendons inward, creating chi pressure.

2. Simultaneously pull up your genitals, closing your anus, and pinch your elbow joints tightly to help create more chi pressure. Exhaling in this manner creates pressure and a slight tension that will torque all the tendons of the body.

3. Upon inhalation, relax and gently breath in, releasing all the different pressures that have been created.

⊙ Coordinating the Heartbeat, Breath, and Movements

Once you have mastered these movements and they are familiar to you, you are ready to coordinate them with the all-important rhythm of your heartbeat and your exhalations. As mentioned earlier, Taoists believe that the heart controls the movement of the tendons (fig. 5.11). When the heart contracts, the tendons gently contract (fig. 5.12), and when it expands, they release this very subtle tension and expand. Based on this knowledge, Taoists stress the vital importance of coordinating the

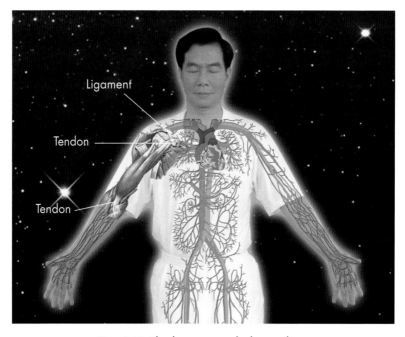

Ligament

Tendon

Tendon

Fig. 5.11 The heart controls the tendons.

Fig. 5.12. Position when the heart contracts

contraction of the heart with the torquing of the tendons and pulling up of the sexual organs. Timing the movement with the heartbeat greatly assists in bringing earth force through the tendons and is a vital aspect of Tendon Nei Kung.

Ultimately you need to be moving to the exact beat of your heart. Exhaling, you will rock forward onto your toes, stretching your finger tendons and pulling up your sexual organs in coordination with the expansion of your heart (peristaltic beat). Inhaling, you will rock back onto your heels, releasing all the tension in your body, in coordination with the contraction of your heart. In order to do this, though, you need to have a strong sense of the heart's pulsing.

Sensing the heart's pulse is more challenging than most people expect, especially when they attempt to do it during physical movement. Even when you have the necessary meditation experience, when the heart is relatively relaxed, as it should be when you are practicing Tendon Nei Kung, its beat may at first be too subtle to register consciously. However, with a little practice you will soon be able to sense your heartbeat in just about any situation.

○ Sensing the Heart's Rhythm

1. Sit down and arrange yourself in a relaxed meditative position. Go into your heart with your mind. Smile down to your heart and see to what extent you can sense its contractions and expansions.

2. If you find that you cannot pick up its rhythm whatsoever, place your middle and index fingers across your palm to feel your pulse. Keeping your mind in your heart, try as best you can to feel in your heart the rhythm you feel in your palm. Once you think you have a good sense of the rhythm, try again to sense the heart's pulse with out the aid of your palm.

3. If you find that you are still unable to feel your heartbeat on its own, make use of your palm to feel your pulse until you think you are ready to do it without using your palm. By continuing in this way you will soon be able to sense your heart's pulse with your mind.

Once you feel that you have more or less mastered the ability to sense your heartbeat, you may try to do the forms in accordance with your heartbeat. It may be easiest to try this first from a sitting position, starting the movement from the base of the spine and ending in the fingers, as there will be less movement to distract you.

Once you can coordinate your forms with your heartbeat in a sitting position, it should be easy to advance to a standing position. By practicing in coordination with your heartbeat in this way, you will be able to grow your tendons much more effectively.

○ Internalizing

Start with reasonably large and animated external movements. Familiarize yourself with the internal force that is generated when you execute the movements correctly. What does the earth force feel like? Once you have a deep practice—you can execute all the internal and external movements as if they were second nature and you can generate the force—you can then attempt to internalize the movements.

There should always be some visible external movement, but once you feel you are ready you should limit the external movements as much as possible while still being able to feel the internal force. If you attempt to limit the movements but don't feel the same internal force generated by your previous larger movements, this is a clear indication that you are not yet ready to internalize the movements. In this case it will be necessary for you to spend more time practicing before reattempting the internalization of the movements.

❂ The Importance of the Eyes

Being visually oriented, human beings rely heavily on their eyesight. Because of this we direct huge amounts of our chi with our eyes, consciously or unconsciously. The Taoists were well aware of this and thought of the eyes as the windows of the soul. They knew that unless we greatly lack concentrated mental focus, our mind generally goes where our senses (and primarily our vision) go. Based on this knowledge, they realized that the eyes could be of great aid in Chi Kung exercise as an aid in directing chi to specific areas. In Tendon Nei Kung the eyes can play an important role in directing chi. As the heart expands and we exhale from the tan tien, we can greatly help direct chi to our fingers by expanding our eyes as much as possible and focusing on our hands and fingers with a strong intent (fig. 5.13).

Fig. 5.13. Directing chi with the eyes by expanding them

Concentrating on Individual Fingers

All the tendons connect in the fingers. By emphasizing tendon work in individual fingers, we can greatly strengthen a specific line of tendons (fig. 5.14).

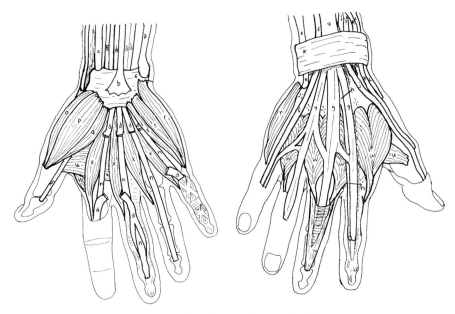

Fig. 5.14. Tendon lines ending in the fingers

The Eight Hand and Arm Positions of Tendon Nei Kung

Once you have developed the basic structure of the Tendon Nei Kung forms in the Iron Shirt Chi Kung stance and you are confident with the movements and various details, you are ready to advance your practice by making use of the eight hand and arm positions.

By practicing the eight positions you strengthen and grow all of the various tendons in the body. Consistently practicing in this way will greatly strengthen your tendons as a unit, instead of having one line of tendons being more developed than another, leaving the others to become weak.

🌀 The First Position

1. Keeping your hands relaxed, hold them at nose level, with the palms facing inward, in a fashion similar to the Iron Shirt position (fig. 5.15).

2. Following the movements described earlier in this chapter for the basic structure, bring the earth's force up through your body.

3. As your heart expands and you exhale to your tan tien and torque your tendons from the ankles up, open up your scapulae and sink your chest, in this way moving your arm structure forward 1 to 1½ feet. (Remember that the apparent movement of the arms in Tendon Nei Kung and Tài Chi forms is, in reality, only a result of the sinking of the chest and the opening of the scapulae. Do not use the muscles in your arms!)

4. As your arms move forward, torque the tendons in your hands. Very gently open and stretch your hands, emphasizing the tensing of the tendons in your middle fingers.

Fig. 5.15. First position

5. Expand your eyes and use your visual focus and mental awareness to direct and sense the earth's force pulse into your finger tendons.

⊙ The Second Position

1. Hold your hands at eye level, with your palms facing each other, creating an upside-down V or roof shape (fig. 5.16).
2. Following the movements described earlier in this chapter for the basic structure, bring the earth's force up through your body.
3. As your heart expands and you exhale to your tan tien and torque the tendons from the ankles up, move your arm structure about 1 foot away from your body, keeping your hands at eye level. As you do this, direct your visual focus and mental awareness primarily toward your pinkie fingers.
4. Gently stretch and tense all the finger tendons, charging them with the earth's force, while emphasizing the pinkie-finger tendons.

Fig. 5.16. Second position

🌀 The Third Position

1. Hold your hands at the level of your abdomen, with your palms facing each other, as though you were holding a soccer ball (fig. 5.17).
2. Following the movements described earlier in this chapter for the basic structure, bring the earth's force up through your body.
3. As your heart expands and you exhale to your tan tien and torque the tendons from your ankles up, move your arm structure directly forward 1 to 1½ feet, keeping your hands at the level of your abdomen, and gently open and stretch your four fingers forward, away from your body. At the same time, direct your visual focus and mental awareness toward your thumbs and gently stretch them up toward the heavens.
4. Feel the earth's force spread into your fingers, especially the thumbs.

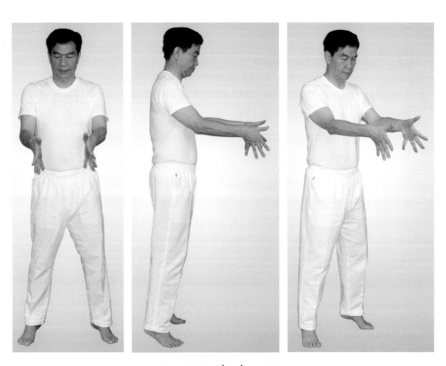

Fig. 5.17. Third position

Fig. 5.18. Fourth position

The Fourth Position

1. Hold your hands at the level of your abdomen, with your palms facing the ground (fig. 5.18).
2. Following the movements described earlier in this chapter for the basic structure, bring the earth's force up through your body.
3. As your heart expands and you torque your tendons from the ankles up, move your arms up and out as chi travels through them. At the same time direct your visual focus and mental awareness to the tops of your hands; feel the chi rising up and moving out through the tops of your hands.
4. Cultivate a feeling of resistance to downward force, as though someone were leaning on the tops of your hands. Your hands need move only about ½ foot both up and out.

☀ The Fifth Position

1. Hold your hands 1½ to 2 feet in front of your solar plexus. Make a V or roof shape with your hands, similar to the second position, but with a less acute angle (fig. 5.19). Keep your elbows down and relaxed. An easy way to find the correct position is to take up the basic Iron Shirt Chi Kung stance with your hands about 2 feet out from your solar plexus level. From this position, simply turn your inward-facing hands to face at an angle to the ground.

2. Following the movements described earlier in this chapter for the basic structure, bring the earth's force up through your body.

3. As your heart expands and you torque your tendons from the ankles up, move your arms about 1 foot away from your body, keeping your hands at the level of the solar plexus. At the same time direct your visual focus and mental awareness to the pinkie fingers, tensing them slightly to charge them with chi.

4. Feel the earth's force pulse into your finger tendons, with emphasis on the pinkie fingers.

Fig. 5.19. Fifth position

❂ *The Sixth Position*

1. Hold your hands at shoulder level, about 1 foot away from your body, with your palms facing your chest (fig. 5.20). Keep your elbows down and relaxed.

2. Following the movements described earlier in this chapter for the basic structure, bring the earth's force up and through your body.

3. As your heart expands and you torque your tendons from the ankles up, move your arms forward, up, and out about ½ foot. Make your arm and hand movements larger and more animated than in the previous forms. As your arms move, slightly raise your elbows, but make sure you do not lift them over the height of your hands.

4. Direct your visual focus to your hands and fingers, and bring your mental awareness to the movement of the spine, emphasizing its whiplike motion and feeling it being charged with the earth's force.

Fig. 5.20. Sixth position

☯ The Seventh Position

1. Hold your hands at waist level, with your palms facing up and the fingers of each hand pointing toward those of the other, creating the shape of a basket (fig. 5.21).
2. Following the movements described earlier in this chapter for the basic structure, bring the earth's force up and through your body.
3. As your heart expands and you torque your tendons from the ankles up, move your arm structure forward and slightly up about 1 to 1½ feet. Again, focus on your spine and emphasize moving it like a whip.
4. Direct your visual focus to your hands and fingers, and bring your mental awareness to the movement of the spine, feeling it being charged with the earth's force.

Fig. 5.21. Seventh position

✑ The Eighth Position

1. Hold your hands at knee level, only a couple of inches away from your knees, with your palms facing upward (fig. 5.22). To reach knee level with your hands you will need to bend your knees more than in any of the previous positions. Bend over your toes and keep your back straight! Do not cheat yourself by arching your spine to reach your knees, as this will simply neutralize any of the desired effects of this form.

2. While squatting, follow the movements as described earlier in this chapter for the basic structure to bring the earth's force up and through your body.

3. As your heart expands and you exhale to your tan tien and torque your tendons from the ankles up, straighten your knees until they are bent only slightly.

4. At the same time, move your arm structure forward and slightly up, allowing your arms to swing like a pendulum, expanding out to create a basket shape. Move each arm from the scapula and shoulder as a unit, without adjusting at any of the arm joints, while at the same time turning your hands outward to torque the arm, hand, and finger tendons.

Fig. 5.22. Eighth position

5. Direct your visual focus to your hands and fingers, directing the earth's force to them. Emphasize the spine moving like a whip and use your mental awareness to feel the spine being charged with the earth's force.

 ## Tai Chi Chi Kung Stance Application

Once you are familiar with the various movements and principles of the Tendon Nei Kung forms, you can start adapting the movements to your Tai Chi Chi Kung form. To start doing this you can use the push position.

1. Stand with your hands out in front of your body at about shoulder height, with your elbows down, and with one leg forward. Rest about 70 percent of your weight on your front foot, as in the Bow and Arrow stance (fig. 5.23). This is the push position.

Fig. 5.23. Tendon Nei Kung movement in the Tai Chi Bow and Arrow stance

2. The first step is to initiate movement from below. To do this, first shift your weight from your front leg to your back leg. As soon as your weight has shifted to the back leg, project your weight back to the front leg. If done correctly this movement should encourage your spine to move like a whip, as in the Tendon Nei Kung forms.

   Practice this basic movement for a while, doing the movement at least a few thousand times, concentrating only on the leg movement. You will slowly begin to feel the power that can be generated by this movement move from your legs to your tailbone and up your spine. Do not expect that after just one or two days of this practice you will be able to feel the power being generated. In ancient times people would spend 20 years doing only this movement, but when they pushed someone, that person would fly. (Such a course of practice does not, of course, have to be equaled, but it is a good indicator that this movement is worth some time and attention.)

3. Once you can feel the force rising up through your legs to your spine, start concentrating on tucking in the sacrum and pushing out the lumbar spine. Again, isolate this movement and practice it for a while, concentrating on the sacrum and lumbar movement until you can do it in your sleep.

4. Once you can feel the power being generated by the movement of the sacrum and lumbar spine, you can advance the movement to pushing out the eleventh thoracic vertebra (T11). Again, practice this sequence of movement (the leg movement, the tucking of the sacrum and pushing out of the lumbar, and the pushing out of T11) until it is second nature.

5. Once you feel that you have mastered the movement of T11 you can again advance, this time adding the pushing out of the area of the heart chakra, between the scapulae. As the power comes up through the sacrum, lumbar spine, and T11 and reaches the area between the scapulae, push out this area of the spine and widen the scapulae, simultaneously hollowing your chest. Practice this movement until you have mastered it.

6. The next area is the seventh cervical vertebra (C7) at the base of the neck. As the power comes up to this area, push out the base of the neck, tucking in your chin. The result of this movement is that your neck and head move forward with the whiplike motion being generated by the spine. As in the Tendon Nei Kung forms, the pushing out of C7 and the neck and the tucking in of the chin should be timed to coincide with the climax of the movement, that is, when the actual push manifests in your hands.

Keep in mind that the apparent hand and arm movement that is used to push is, in reality, only the result of the movement of pushing out the scapulae. If you literally push with your arms, you will lose your structure and the internal force will be almost completely useless.

Once you have grasped this entire whiplike movement of the spine in the Tai Chi Chi Kung stance, you can add the other facets of the Tendon Nei Kung movements, pulling up the sexual organs and flattening the stomach, pressing the tongue to the palate, and exhaling to your tan tien to generate maximum internal force. The eight hand movements of the Tendon Nei Kung forms can also be practiced out of the Bow and Arrow Tai Chi Chi Kung stance.

GENERAL INFORMATION ABOUT TENDON NEI KUNG

When practicing the basic Tendon Nei Kung movements and the movements out of the Tai Chi Chi Kung stance, it is necessary for you to really make use of your awareness to "feel" your tendons. Torque each tendon and follow the gentle tension with highest awareness. If your mind is distracted and busy with other things, the practice will not deliver high-quality benefits. Feel the tendons torque against your bone structure, stretching and strengthening them at each level up your body. Use your awareness to sense the powerful healing energy of the earth move through your body from the bottom up: toes, heels, ankles, legs, hips, spinal cord, Jade Pillow (base of the skull), arms, and finally the fingers.

Once you are completely familiar with this motion and can execute the entire sequence without having to consciously think about it, the movement should take no longer than half a second from the toes to the fingers when done at a normal speed with a sense of confidence. Naturally, when you are familiarizing yourself with the external and internal movements you should work as slowly as is necessary for you to perform all the steps while still adhering to all the vital principles. Do not be in a rush to do the entire form at full speed.

It is possible to practice the form correctly from an external perspective but not from an internal one. If you do not carefully adhere to all the internal and mental principles of the form, you risk losing a lot of the potential gain that awaits the dedicated student. In studying Tendon Nei Kung, proceed carefully and patiently, making sure you include every last one of the above-mentioned details. Study, practice, and feel. You will know that you are doing it correctly when it feels correct.

Tendon Nei Kung Partner Forms

The efficiency of the tendon strengthening exercises can be tested and increased by doing the forms with a partner. In this training the weight of the partner is used to engage the tendons of the practitioner. The practitioner then uses a quick stretch of the tendons to bounce the partner's energy back. This exercise should be performed in a gentle, repetitive manner, without reverting to brute force to bounce the partner.

Make sure you have mastered the basic principles and have a relatively deep practice of the individual forms before moving on to the partner exercises. If you have not cultivated a good sense of what the internal force feels like, prematurely moving on to the partner forms will invariably cause you to use muscle force to attempt to bounce your partner back, resulting in a useless exercise.

The principles of movement for the practitioner remain exactly the same as in the solo forms. The eight positions that are used in the solo forms are also used for training with a partner.

Your partner must be sensitive to you and adjust according to your capability. It is not necessary for your partner to lean all his or her weight on you. The idea is for your partner to gently lean into you, trying to sense where your limit is without knocking you off balance. As you become more confident and competent with the partner forms, your partner can slowly increase the momentum of his or her leaning to help gradually increase your power. Your partner should be more or less the same size and weight as you. It's by no means crucial if there is a slight difference in weight or height, but a ten-year-old child would not be a suitable partner for a 150-pound grown man, for example.

Eight Positions for Working with a Partner

General Procedure with a Partner

Have your partner stand up straight with his feet together, facing you, about a meter away. From this position let him put his hands on your wrists and then lean into you. In return you will meet his oncoming momentum by shifting your body into alignment with his force and the earth so that you can root his force and also channel earth force. When you first begin this practice your countering movement will cause you to lean forward ever so slightly, no more than a degree or two, but once you get a feeling for the practice you can internalize the movement until there is no apparent external shifting or leaning forward (fig. 6.1).

At this stage it is important to make sure that you are not using force to resist your partner's momentum. You must resist relying on muscle power to receive your partner's force without being knocked over. However, when we say "don't use force" we don't mean that you must be totally weak, so that you could be pushed by a sudden breeze. The way to receive your partner's force is to absorb and store his force in all of your tendons, from your arms and shoulders, down your back, through your Achilles tendons, and into your toes, rooting out any excess force through your heels. To do this it is necessary to lock and engage in the structure of the Tendon Nei Kung form, especially the

Fig. 6.1.
Partner practice

arms, with the joints and tendons. Once you are storing your partner's energy, you can use the Tendon Nei Kung form movement and your awareness (mind, eye, and heart) to return that force and bounce your partner. As you bounce him, lift and expand your toes to further torque the tendons of your body.

As you repulse your partner he must grab on to your wrists so that he is not pushed away completely. He can then pull himself back and lean into you again so that the process may be repeated. Doing this will help you practice quick, rhythmic repetitions. Start your practice with about ten repetitions for each hand position, and then, if you like, increase your practice as your ability increases.

Fig. 6.2. The first position with a partner

❂ The First Position with a Partner

1. Assume the first position, bringing your hands to nose level with the palms facing inward, and let your partner lean on your wrists (fig. 6.2).
2. As your partner leans in, very slightly lean forward to meet and absorb his momentum.
3. Absorb and store his energy in your tendons, while rooting excess energy out of your heels.
4. Using the Tendon Nei Kung principles and movements, torque your tendons from the ankles up, bouncing your partner. Remember to emphasize the stretching of the tendons in the middle fingers.

❂ The Second Position with a Partner

1. Assume the second position, with your hands forming the shape of a roof, and let your partner lean on your wrists (fig. 6.3).
2. As your partner leans in, very slightly lean forward to meet and absorb his oncoming momentum.

Fig. 6.3. Second position with a partner

3. Absorb and store his energy in your tendons, while rooting excess energy out of your heels.
4. Using the Tendon Nei Kung movements and principles, torque and stretch your tendons to bounce your partner. Lift and expand your toes to help stretch the tendons for more power, assisting you in repelling your partner. Remember to emphasize the stretching of the pinkie tendons for this position.

❂ The Third Position with a Partner

1. Take up the third position, extending your hands as if they were holding a soccer ball in front of your abdomen, and have your partner lean on the thumb side of your wrists (fig. 6.4).
2. As your partner leans in, very slightly lean forward to meet his oncoming momentum.
3. Absorb and store his energy in your tendons, while rooting excess energy out of your heels.
4. Use the Tendon Nei Kung movements and principles to torque and stretch your tendons, bouncing your partner. Keep your elbows well bent and extend your power from your shoulders and through the locked elbows, letting your force move up and out.

❂ The Fourth Position with a Partner

1. Take up the fourth position, with your palms facing down, and have your partner lean on the tops of your wrists (fig. 6.5 on page 70).
2. As your partner leans in, very slightly lean forward to meet and absorb his oncoming momentum.
3. Absorb and store his energy in your tendons, while rooting excess energy out of your heels.
4. Using the Tendon Nei Kung movements and principles, torque and stretch your tendons, bouncing your partner. Feel the chi rising up and lifting out of the backs of your hands to repel your partner.

❂ The Fifth Position with a Partner

1. Take up the fifth position, with your hands at the level of the solar plexus forming the shape of a roof, and have your partner lean on the fronts of your wrists (fig. 6.6 on page 71).
2. As your partner leans in, very slightly lean forward to meet and absorb his oncoming momentum.

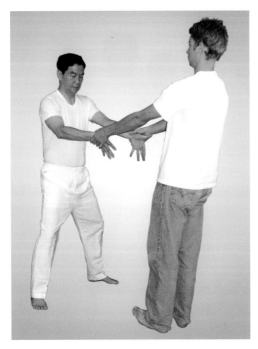

Fig. 6.4. Third position with a partner

Fig. 6.5. Fourth position with a partner

Fig. 6.6. Fifth position with a partner

3. Using the Tendon Nei Kung movements and principles, torque and stretch your tendons, bouncing your partner. Remember to emphasize the stretching of the pinkie-finger tendons, and make use of the spine's whiplike movement to generate force for repelling your partner.

The Sixth Position with a Partner

1. Take up the sixth position, with your palms facing you, in the basic Iron Shirt stance (fig. 6.7). Have your partner lean on the spot where the thumb bone meets the wrist.
2. As your partner leans in, very slightly lean forward to meet and absorb his oncoming momentum.
3. Absorb and store his energy in your tendons, while rooting excess energy out of your heels.
4. Using the Tendon Nei Kung movements and principles, torque and stretch your tendons to bounce your partner. Remember to emphasize moving the spine like a whip to generate force for repelling your partner.

The Seventh Position with a Partner

1. Take up the seventh position, with your hands at waist height and fingers pointing toward each other, forming a basket (fig. 6.8 on page 74). Have your partner lean on the spot where the thumb bone meets the wrist.
2. As your partner leans in, very slightly lean forward to meet and absorb his oncoming momentum.
3. Absorb and store his energy in your tendons, while rooting excess energy out of your heels.
4. Using the Tendon Nei Kung movements and principles, torque and stretch your tendons to bounce your partner. For this position be sure to lock your shoulder joints under your partner's force before repelling him, and emphasize the whiplike motion of the spinal cord to create extra bouncing force.

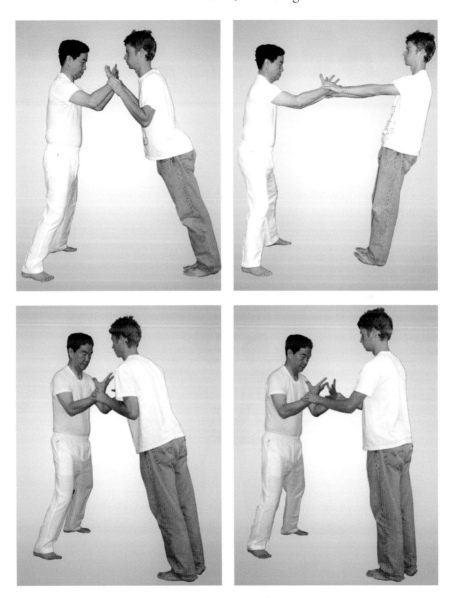

Fig. 6.7. Sixth position with a partner

Fig. 6.8. Seventh position with a partner

Fig. 6.9. Eighth position with a partner

❂ The Eighth Position with a Partner

1. Take up the eighth position, with your knees bent and your hands at knee level, forming a basket with your fingers (fig. 6.9). Have your partner place his hands on your shoulders.
2. As your partner leans in, very slightly sink down and forward with your legs to meet and absorb his oncoming momentum.
3. Absorb and store his energy in your tendons, while rooting excess energy out of your heels.
4. Using the Tendon Nei Kung movements and principles, torque and stretch your tendons, bouncing your partner. For this position, emphasize moving the spine like a whip and try to sense the earth's force pulsing through your spine.

⊙ Closing Movements for Partner Practice

1. Once you have finished your partner practice, shake your body out well, loosening it up after the physical contact.
2. Relax and smile to all your tendons, using your awareness to guide the healing energy to them.
3. Stand up straight, with your feet together and your hands over your tan tien. Men should place their right hand over their left, and women their left over their right.
4. Stand in this way for several minutes, breathing calmly and collecting and storing the energy at your tan tien (fig. 6.10).

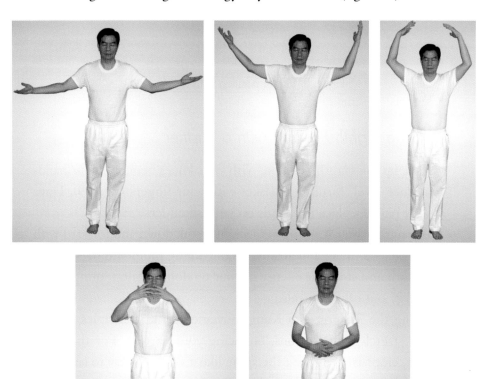

Fig. 6.10. Closing movements for partner practice

Wall Practice

Often enough it is not easy to find someone who is about your size and willing to spend ten to twenty minutes a day to do the Tendon Nei Kung partner practices. In this case you can make use of a wall to test and increase your Tendon Nei Kung "bouncing" ability (fig. 6.11).

In practicing with a wall, all the body and hand positions and principles remain exactly the same as in the solo forms, except that some of the positions are excluded because they are not possible to do with a wall.

General Procedure for Wall Practice

1. Stand at about an arm's length away from the wall.
2. Fall against the wall slowly, and using the same principles as for the solo forms, bounce yourself back to your original position by stretching your tendons.
3. Do the movements repetitively, starting with just a few repetitions and gradually building up your practice to ten repetitions for each position.

Fig. 6.11. Wall practice

❂ First Position with a Wall

1. Assume the first position of the solo forms, with your arms at head level and palms facing in. Lean into the wall, with the backs of your hands and wrists making contact with the wall (fig. 6.12). Keep your muscles relaxed, allowing your tendons to engage and absorb your momentum's force.
2. Expand your toes and use the Tendon Nei Kung movements and principles to torque and stretch your tendons, bouncing yourself off the wall and back to your original upright position.

❂ Second Position with a Wall

1. Assume the second position, with your arms at head level and your hands forming the peak of a roof shape (fig. 6.13). Lean into the wall, making contact with the pinkie sides of your hands. Keep your muscles relaxed, allowing your tendons to engage and absorb your momentum's force.
2. Expand your toes and use the Tendon Nei Kung movements and principles to torque and stretch your tendons, bouncing yourself off the wall. Emphasize the stretching of the pinkie tendons.

❂ Third Position with a Wall
(Fifth Position of Solo Forms)

1. Assume the fifth position of the solo forms, making a roof shape with your hands at the level of your solar plexus (fig. 6.14). Lean into the wall, making contact with the pinkie sides of your hands. Keep your muscles relaxed, allowing your tendons to engage and absorb your momentum's force.
2. Expand your toes and use the Tendon Nei Kung movements and principles to torque and stretch your tendons, bouncing yourself off the wall. Emphasize the stretching of your pinkie tendons.

Fig. 6.12. First
position with a
wall

Fig. 6.13. Second
position with a
wall

Fig. 6.14 Third
position with a wall
(fifth position of the
solo forms)

☯ Fourth Position with a Wall
(Sixth Position of Solo Forms)

1. Assume the sixth position of the solo forms, with your hands at shoulder level (fig. 6.15). Lean into the wall, making contact with the backs of your hands. Keep your muscles relaxed, engaging your tendons to absorb and store your momentum's force.

2. Expand your toes and use the Tendon Nei Kung movements and principles to torque and stretch your tendons, bouncing yourself off the wall and back to your original position. Try to really sense your tendons' elasticity working for you and your whole body feeling like rubber. Emphasize moving your spine like a whip and feel it being charged with chi.

☯ Fifth Position with a Wall
(Seventh Position of Solo Forms)

1. Assume the seventh position of the solo forms (fig. 6.16). Lean into the wall, making contact with the backs of your wrists at waist level. Keep your muscles relaxed, engaging your tendons to absorb and store your momentum's force.

2. Expand your toes and use the Tendon Nei Kung movements and principles to torque and stretch your tendons, bouncing yourself off the wall and back to your original position. Emphasize moving the spine like a whip and feel it being charged with chi.

☯ Closing Movements for Wall Practice

1. Once you have finished your wall practice, shake your body out well, loosening it up after the physical contact.

2. Relax and smile to all your tendons, using your awareness to guide the healing energy to them.

Fig. 6.15. Fourth position with a wall
(sixth position of the solo forms)

Fig. 6.16. Fifth position with a wall
(seventh position of the solo forms)

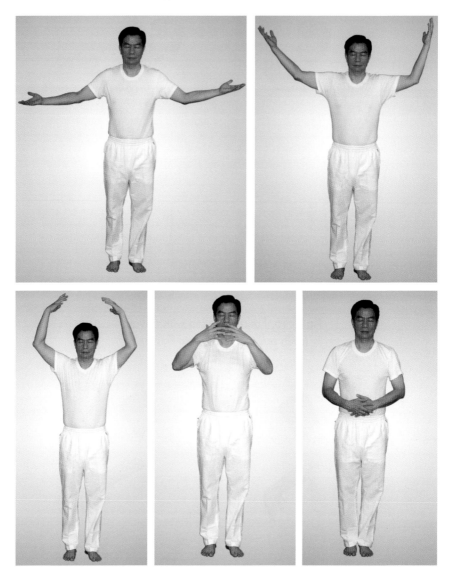

Fig. 6.17. Closing movements for wall practice

3. Stand up straight, with your feet together and your hands over your tan tien. Men should place their right hand over their left, and women their left hand over their right.
4. Stand in this way for several minutes, breathing calmly and collecting and storing the energy at your tan tien (fig. 6.17).

Ten Supplementary Tendon Exercises

The supplementary exercises concentrate specifically on strengthening, stretching, and loosening up the tendons and joints without strenuous movement. The supplementary exercises can also be used to help heal damaged tendons and joints.

 ## Ten Supplementary Exercises

Supplemental Exercise 1: Punching Out of the Mouth

The Punching Out of the Mouth tendon-stretching exercise is extremely effective for strengthening tendons, but it is also a vicious attack technique from Wu Fu and may come in use for martial arts practitioners (see fig. 7.1 on pages 85 and 86 and fig. 7.2 on page 87). For this reason using the hips is crucial. As in almost all worthwhile martial arts, power is generated from the hips.

1. Stand with your left leg one long step forward and half a step to the left of your right leg (a).
2. Slowly make an uppercut punching motion with your right hand, twisting your fist clockwise as far as it can possibly go. As you do this, thrust your hips in, squaring them as much as possible. Pull your left hand back to your hip, also clenching it into a fist. Really stretch out in this manner, exhaling slowly and power-fully (b, c).
3. Now untwist your fist and open it into a claw, unsquaring your hips (d). Imagine an opponent's face in front of you and claw down over his face from top to bottom, squaring your hips (e). When clawing down it is important not to use just your arm strength. Instead, use your whole body weight to sink down from the legs. In this way if you weigh 70 kilograms, you will have 70 kilograms of clawing force. If you use only your arm power, though, you will do well to generate just 20 kilograms of force.
4. Now grab the imaginary face by the lip and nose and twist clock-wise as far as you can, while unsquaring your hips to generate force into the move (f).
5. Without releasing your relentless grip on your opponent's face, pull your gripping hand down to your hip (g on page 86). When you do this, shift your weight to your back leg and sink down from your hips and knees to pull down your imaginary opponent with your full body weight.
6. Without changing your leg position, now use your other arm to attack in this manner, following the same principles of twisting your hips and arms together (h–l on page 86).
7. After changing arms several times, change legs and go through the series of movements again, now with your right leg in front.

Opposite. Fig. 7.1. Punching Out of the Mouth

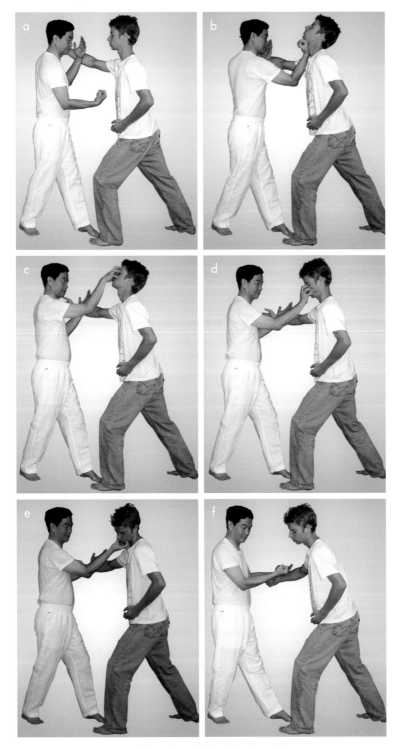

Fig. 7.2. Punching Out of the Mouth with a partner

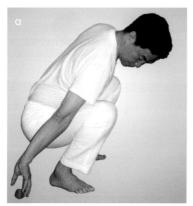 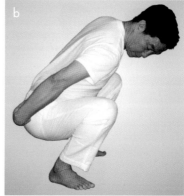

Fig. 7.3. Picking Up the Stone

❂ Supplemental Exercise 2: Picking Up the Stone

This exercise stretches and strengthens not only the tendons in the arms but also those in the legs. Do your best to really sink low into your stance so that you would be able to pick up that imaginary stone. If you practice like this consistently your thigh and calf muscles will become greatly strengthened, and more importantly your leg and groin tendons will be greatly stretched and strengthened (fig. 7.3).

1. Squat with your feet in a line about two shoulder widths apart. Make a fist with your left hand and place the back of your left forearm on your hip. Use your right hand to pretend to pick up a stone just behind your right ankle (a).
2. Twist your wrist and arm clockwise as far as they can go, in this way stretching the arm tendons (b).
3. Carry the stone across your hip (c) and set it down in front of your right leg, near your ankle, again twisting your arm in a clockwise direction (d).
4. Pick up the stone again (e, f) and put it back behind your right ankle (g, h), repeating the twisting motion with your arm, this time in a counterclockwise direction.
5. Change hands and repeat the procedure on your left side.

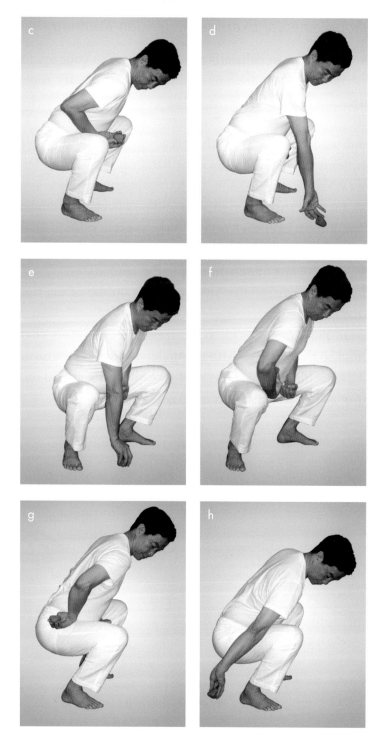

✿ *Supplemental Exercise 3: Tendon Rubbing*

This exercise assists in cultivating more strength in your tendons and involves rubbing your forearms against each other with some force (fig. 7.4).

1. Stand with your feet slightly spread out in a comfortable position, with the back of your right hand on top of your left forearm (a).
2. Push forward with the right arm and pull back with the left arm, scraping them over each other slowly, causing substantial friction between the two forearms (b). As you rub them together in this way, stretch your fingers to torque the tendons.
3. Now switch arms, so that the left arm is on top of the right, and do the same.
4. Repeat the rubbing with both arms, now twisting your arms around so that you rub with the underside of your forearm (c, d), and then with your palm on your forearm (e, f), and so on. Carry on for as long as you feel is necessary.

Fig. 7.4. Tendon Rubbing

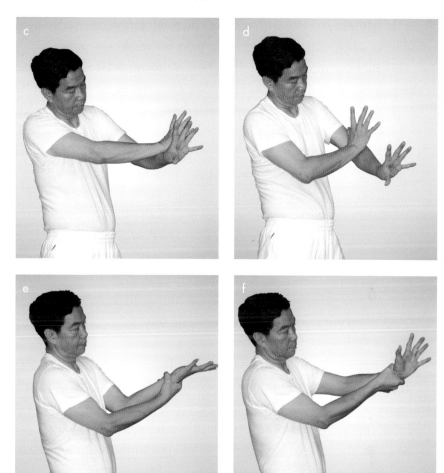

🜚 Supplemental Exercise 4: Finger Flicking

The motion performed with your arms, hands, and fingers is similar to that of flicking a dry cloth. The essence of this exercise is simply a flick or a snap of the hands and fingers (see fig. 7.5 on page 93).

Throughout the exercise, remember to inhale when you rise from your knees and raise your arms and to exhale when you sink and flick.

Treat this simple exercise with respect and moderation, as overdoing it could leave unconditioned tendons in pain for weeks on end.

This flicking practice is highly effective for martial arts practice. If you practice with dedication for a few years, you can easily generate more power with a flick than with a full-force punch.

1. Stand with your feet a little more than shoulder width apart, in a comfortable position, and bend your knees.
2. Inhale, rise from your knees, and bring your hands up the middle of your body, with your elbows bent and the backs of the hands facing each other, keeping them as relaxed as possible (a, b).
3. As your hands rise above your head, exhale sharply, bend from the knees, and flick your hands and fingers as though you were shaking off tiny carnivorous fish that are biting the ends of your fingers. Keep your arms relaxed the whole way, tensing only slightly as you flick (c).
4. Let your arms and hands gently sink down to waist level, relaxing them totally and letting them hang loosely by your sides for a moment.
5. Now repeat the motion, except this time let your hands come down to about head level before exhaling and flicking them (d).
6. Again, let your arms and hands gently sink down to waist level, relaxing them totally, and let them hang loosely by your sides for a moment.
7. Repeat this motion again, stretching your arms up and bringing them down gently, and this time flick them as they reach about shoulder height (e, f).
8. Let your arms and hands gently sink down to waist level, relaxing them totally, and let them hang loosely by your sides for a moment.

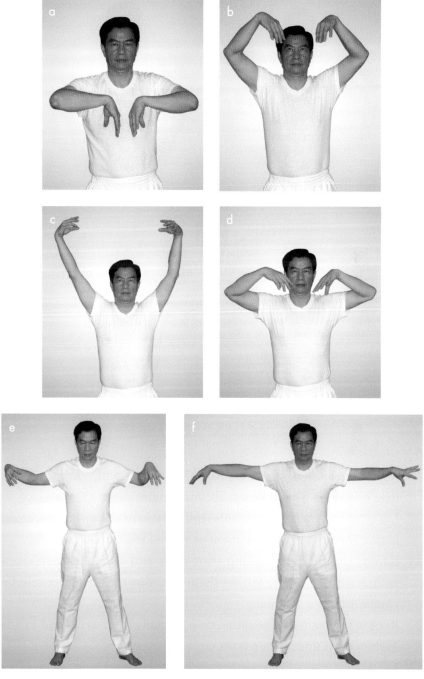

Fig. 7.5. Finger Flicking

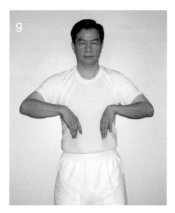

Fig. 7.5. Finger Flicking (cont.)

9. Repeat the motion, stretching your arms up and gently down, and this time give them a good flick as they reach just above waist level (g).

10. Let your arms and hands gently sink the rest of the way down, again letting them relax for a moment at your sides.

11. Repeat the motion, flicking your arms and hands as they reach your waist (h), before letting them sink down to hang loosely by your sides for a moment.

12. Repeat the motion one more time, flicking your arms and hands as they drop under your waist (i).

13. Let your arms and hands hang loosely by your sides now. Give them a good shake, and feel your arm tendons well stretched and loose inside.

☯ *Supplemental Exercise 5: Leg Flicking*

This exercise entails using the same flicking concept that is used for Finger Flicking, except you flick your legs and feet (fig. 7.6). The flicking of the legs, or what can be thought of as kicking, is always lower than knee level for these exercises.

As is the case for Finger Flicking, is important not to do too many repetitions of this flicking exercise, especially when you are doing these practices for the first time.

1. Stand with your feet about shoulder width apart, with your hands on your hips. Exhale and kick forward with a flicking motion, keeping your leg relaxed (a, b, c). Keep the idea of flicking a cloth in mind to help cultivate the correct snapping or flicking feeling.

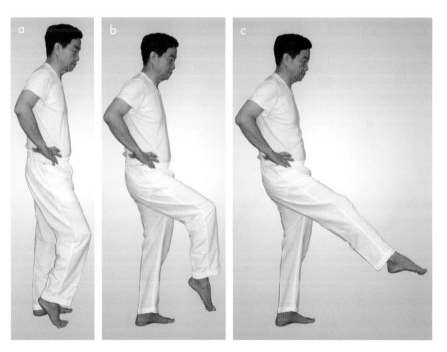

Fig. 7.6. Leg Flicking

2. Then kick in the same manner directly to the side, really snapping your kick as much as possible (d, e, f).
3. Kick in the same manner just behind your body, as though you were kicking a small ball directly behind your leg (g, h, i).
4. Change legs and go through the same routine, kicking to the front, to the side, and behind you with the other leg.
5. Repeat the flicking sequence with each leg in this way a few times.

Fig. 7.6. Leg Flicking (cont.)

✇ *Supplemental Exercise 6: Wrist Twisting*

This exercise entails twisting the wrists and opens and strengthens the tendons and joints in the arms (fig. 7.7).

1. Stand upright with your feet spread about shoulder width apart, in a comfortable position.
2. Hold your arms straight out directly in front of you. Twist both of your wrists inward (the left hand clockwise and the right hand counterclockwise) at the same time, as though you were trying to break the grip of someone holding on to your arm (a, b, c, d, e).

   Each time you spiral your hands and twist your wrists, stretch your arms forward and stretch your lumbar spine out, slightly arching your back, and pull your neck back, as though someone were pushing your head and neck back from your top lip. Do about 10 repetitions in this direction.
3. Now twist your wrists outward (the left hand counterclockwise and the right hand clockwise), again doing about 10 repetitions (f, g, h on page 98).

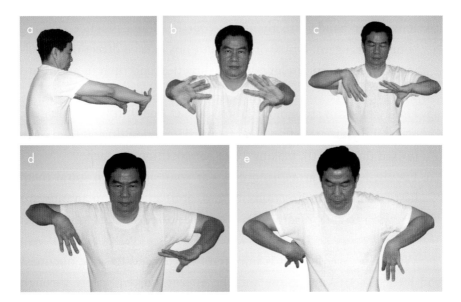

Fig. 7.7. Wrist Twisting

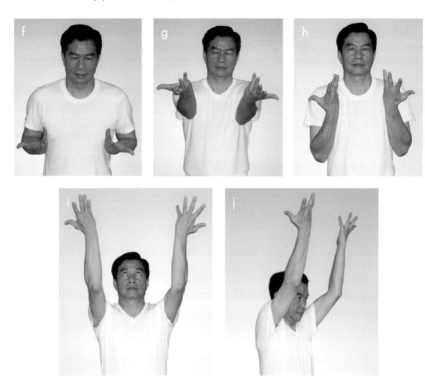

Fig. 7.7. Wrist Twisting (cont.)

4. Raise your hands directly above your head and practice twisting your wrists again. Do 10 or so repetitions in each direction, spiraling your arms first in an outward direction and then in an inward direction (i, j).

5. Hold your arms straight out to the side, in line with your shoulders, and spiral your arms first in an outward direction (k) and then in an inward direction (l), making 10 or so repetitions of each.

6. Finally, let your arms hang down at your sides, then spiral them first in an inward direction (m, n, o, p, q) and then in an outward direction (r, s, t), making 10 or so repetitions of each.

When you are done, it is important to rest and feel the openness and looseness of your joints and the energy pulsing freely through them. Smile to your arm tendons and use your awareness to absorb the chi into your tendons.

Fig. 7.8. Opening the Lumbar Spine

☀ Supplemental Exercise 7: Opening the Lumbar Spine

This exercise helps open the all-important lumbar spine and the neck as well as stretching the various tendons in the back and neck (fig. 7.8).

1. Stand with your legs straight and your feet spread about two shoulder widths apart.
2. Hold the thumb of one hand with your other hand, and stretch your arms up above your head as far as possible (a).
3. Keeping your arms stretched out above your head, exhale slowly and powerfully and stretch forward and then down, so that your hands touch the ground—according to your capabilities, of course (b, c, d).

4. Now inhale and bring your hands back up along the middle of your body (e, f).
5. At the top of your inhalation, stretch back up above your head and arch your back backward as far as is comfortable (g).
6. Do a few repetitions of this stretch, and then reverse your hands and repeat.
7. Next, raise your hands above your head in the same way. Twist your body to face the left while keeping your feet rooted in their position (h). It is very important that you twist your body from the hips.
8. Exhale, and stretch up and then down toward the ground (i, j).

Fig. 7.8. Opening the Lumbar Spine (cont.)

9. Touch the ground with your hands, bending your knees if necessary (k).
10. Swing your arms and body around from the left side to the right side, turning from the hips (l).
11. Once you have turned as far to the right as you can, bring your arms up, keeping your hips twisted to the right, and arch your back (m, n, o).
12. Come back down and touch the ground to the right (p, q, r).
13. Swing your hips to the left and do a few repetitions of the up-and-down movement on the left side (s, t, u) before changing direction and doing several repetitions on the right.
14. Afterward, shake out and smile to the relevant areas.

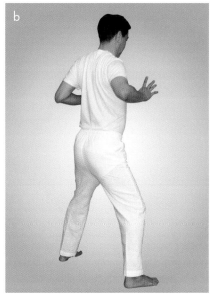

Fig. 7.9. Strengthening the Spinal Cord Tendons

❂ Supplemental Exercise 8: Strengthening the Spinal Cord Tendons

This exercise strengthens the tendons of the spine (fig. 7.9).

1. Stand erect with your legs spread about two shoulder widths apart, slightly bending your knees. Hold your hands in front of your chest, with your palms facing each other, your fingers spread, as though you were holding a soccer ball. Keep your elbows bent and down (a, b).

2. Exhale, and press your hands toward each other as though you were trying to squeeze the air out of the ball.

3. Continue this motion of pressing so that your hands go right past each other. As you do this, sink your chest, tilt your sacrum up, push out your lumbar spine, and curve your back slightly forward while pulling your neck back (c, d). The motion should be

completed at the end of your slow and powerful exhalation, with your hands now about a foot past each other and your fingers stretched out as much as possible.

4. Relax your whole body for a moment, allowing your spine to become erect again.

5. Repeat the exercise 10 or so times, each time changing the hand that is on top.

Once you have the hang of this movement and can feel the tendons in your spine stretching, you can also pull up your sexual organs, pressing in on the abdomen, to help stretch the tendons. Pulling up the sexual organs is very effective in stretching the tendons because the sexual organs themselves are one of the main tendons in the body.

Fig. 7.10. Pushing Down

✿ Supplemental Exercise 9: Pushing Down

The movements in this exercise are almost the same as those for the supplemental exercise 8, Strengthening the Spinal Cord Tendons. The only difference is in the arm and hand position (fig. 7.10).

1. Raise your arms to the level of your forehead and hold them in front of your body, with your palms facing the ground (a, b, c).
2. Exhale, and sink your chest, tilt your sacrum up, push out your lumbar spine, and curve your back slightly forward while pulling your neck back. At the same time, press down with your arms and hands, as though you were attempting to push a log into the ground (d, e, f).
3. Relax your whole body for a moment, allowing your spine to become erect again.
4. Repeat the exercise 10 or so times.

◯ Supplemental Exercise 10: Strengthening the Thumb Tendons

This exercise employs the same movements as supplemental exercises 8 and 9, with the only difference being in the hands (fig. 7.11).

1. Raise your hands to the level of your forehead and clench them into fists, with your thumbs sticking out straight (a, b).
2. Exhale, and sink your chest, tilt your sacrum up, push out your lumbar spine, and curve your back slightly forward while pulling your neck back. At the same time, press your thumbs toward the ground (c). This motion helps strengthen the thumb tendons.
3. Relax your whole body for a moment, allowing your spine to become erect again.
4. Repeat the exercise 10 or so times.

The supplementary exercises should not take the place of the Tendon Nei Kung forms but nevertheless should be practiced diligently whenever time is available. They assist greatly in the strengthening and stretching of the tendons, and when they are combined with the Tendon Nei Kung forms, only the sky is the limit.

Fig. 7.11. Strengthening the Thumb Tendons

Mung Bean Hitting

As result of their intensive and intelligent studies of nature the ancient Taoists discovered many powerful natural medicines and their specific properties. Among their many discoveries was that of the fantastic detoxifying properties of mung beans when applied externally to the body. The Taoists found that mung beans could absorb excess yang energy, which potentially causes overheating or manifestations of poisonous toxins in the body.

The ancient Taoists used mung beans to treat a wide variety of ailments and injuries, reaping many health benefits from them. They found that if any of the internal organs were poisoned, they could greatly assist in detoxification by simple applications of mung beans. They also used mung beans to bring relief in cases of constipation, stomach cramps, and even headaches. However, the ancient Taoists soon discovered that mung beans were especially effective in the repair of damaged tendons and joints and the strengthening of healthy ones. Tendon strengthening soon became the most recognized function of mung bean techniques, and these techniques were often combined with the practice of Tendon Nei Kung for martial arts training and maintaining general health.

APPARATUS: THE MUNG BEAN SOCK

The most convenient and effective way to apply the mung bean heal-ing and strengthening techniques is to place the beans in a cotton sock (fig. 8.1). The mung bean sock is then used in a clublike fashion to firmly hit along the lines of the tendons or other relevant parts of the body meridians. Nylon socks are not suitable for this practice, as nylon quickly stretches from the continual slinging and the beans inevitably spill out, making a fantastic mess.

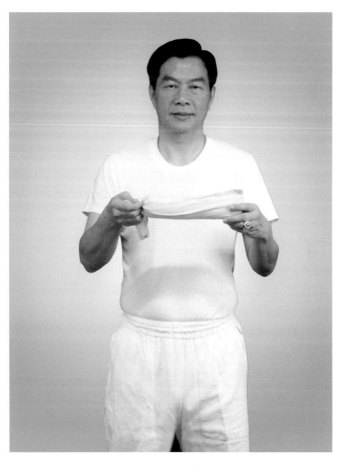

Fig. 8.1. The mung bean sock

Approximately 1 pound has been found to be the optimal amount of mung beans to place in the sock. More or less than a pound of mung beans will prevent you from realizing the optimal intensity of the blows, limiting the success of the techniques.

When you practice Mung Bean Hitting, the hitting should be firm but not extreme. When you first begin this practice, it is appropriate to be a little cautious, so that you don't injure yourself. Once your skin toughens up from consistent practice you can gradually increase the power of your hitting, according to your own discretion.

A sure way to help realize the optimal intensity for your hitting is to simply drop the bean-filled sock onto your arm from a height, without any other added power. This should give you a good indication of the optimal strength with which you can hit yourself. It is advisable to spend a few moments before each session familiarizing yourself with the appropriate strength of your hitting power, which will change over time.

Hitting with Mung Beans: Upper Limbs

The Middle Finger Line

1. Extend your left arm above your shoulder, slightly twisting your arm so that your palm faces up (fig. 8.2). As you twist your arm into place, swallow saliva down into your belly.
2. Start off using the sock to hit the inside of the left elbow 3 times.
3. Continue hitting in a line along the center of the arm to the inside wrist, through the palm, and to the tip of your extended middle finger. Remember to always use your eyes to direct energy to the relevant areas.
4. Return along the same line, continuing on to traverse from the inner elbow to your shoulder and the top of your neck.
5. Follow the same route back to your elbow, giving the joint some final attention.

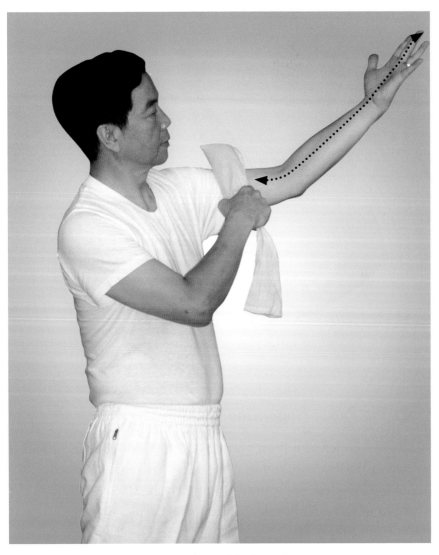

Fig. 8.2. The middle finger line

6. Shake your arm lightly and feel the beaten tendon line more open and loose than before.
7. Rest and smile to the tendon line, using your awareness to help absorb chi into the tendon line.
8. Repeat on the other side.

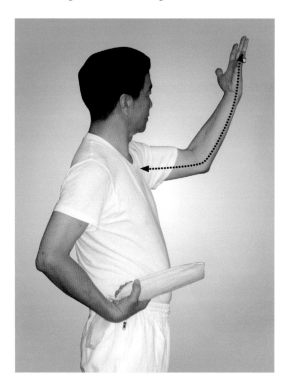

Fig. 8.3. The pinkie finger line

◎ The Pinkie Finger Line

1. Raise your left arm above your shoulder, slightly twisting it so that your palm faces up, and swallow saliva down into your belly.
2. Hit 3 times the point inside the inner left elbow, slightly to the right of its center, where the ulna bone begins.
3. Continue hitting in a line toward the hand, over the lower part of the inner left wrist, to the inside tip of the pinkie finger (fig. 8.3).
4. Return via the same route, continuing up to top of the neck before coming back down to the elbow to give that important joint some final attention.
5. Shake your arm lightly and feel the beaten tendon line more open and loose than before.
6. Rest and smile to the tendon line, using your awareness to help absorb chi into it.
7. Repeat on the other side.

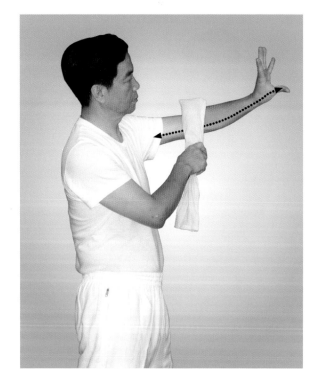

Fig. 8.4. The thumb line

🌀 The Thumb Line

1. Raise your left arm above your shoulder, slightly twisting it so that your palm faces up, and swallow saliva down into your belly.

2. Hit 3 times the point near the outside of the inner elbow, slightly to the left of its center, where the radius bone begins (fig. 8.4).

3. Continue hitting in a line toward the hand, over the upper part of the inner wrist, to the inside tip of the thumb.

4. Return via the same route, continuing up to the top of the neck before coming back down to the elbow to give the joint some final attention.

5. Shake your arm lightly and feel the beaten tendon line more open and loose than before.

6. Rest and smile to the tendon line, using your awareness to help absorb chi into it.

7. Repeat on the other side.

Fig. 8.5. The back
of the hand line

❂ *The Back of the Hand*

1. Extend your arm at about shoulder height.
2. Twist and lower your arm so that the palm faces down, with the pinkie finger pointing toward the sky and the thumb pointing toward the ground (fig. 8.5). At the same time, swallow saliva down into your belly.
3. Hit the point at the top of your elbow.
4. Continue hitting in a line on the top of your arm down to your wrist and then the end of your ring finger.
5. Follow the same route back to the elbow, continuing along the biceps tendon up to the top of the neck before returning to the elbow joint to give it some final attention.
6. Shake your arm lightly and feel the beaten tendon line more open and loose than before.
7. Rest and smile to the tendon line, using your awareness to help absorb chi into the tendon line, replenishing and strengthening it.
8. Repeat on the other side.

Fig. 8.6. The big toe line

 Hitting with Mung Beans: Organs and Lower Limbs

The Big Toe Line

1. Stand with your left leg a good distance forward, well bent and slightly to the side, but without straining yourself. Hold the mung bean sock in your right hand (fig. 8.6). Men should use their left hand to cover their genitals, pulling them out of the way.

2. Swallow saliva down into your belly and start hitting in a line from the left shoulder down the middle line of the body. Hit only softly over the solar plexus, and follow the line in between your abdominal muscles until you reach your tan tien.

3. Continue hitting down the right leg, hitting the inside line of the thigh, down the inside of the knee, and all along the inside of the shinbone and ankle, until you finally reach the big toe.

4. Hit the ankle area 3 additional times, since the spleen, liver, and kidney meridians meet near the ankle on this line.

5. Follow the same route all the way back to the neck.

6. Rest and smile to the tendon line, using your awareness to help absorb chi into the tendon line, replenishing and strengthening it.

7. Repeat on the other side.

Fig. 8.7. The small
toe line

❀ The Small Toe Line

1. Stand with your left leg a good distance forward, well bent and slightly to the side, but without straining yourself. Hold the mung bean sock in your right hand.
2. Raise your left arm in front of your body in a warding-off position, clench your left hand into a fist, and swallow saliva down into your belly.
3. Start hitting under your raised arm, in the armpit, following a straight line down the left flank of your body.
4. Continue hitting down your right leg, hitting the outside of the thigh muscle, past the outside of the knee, all the way down the outside of the calf muscle, and over the ankle, until you reach the small toe (fig. 8.7).
5. Follow the same route all the way back up to the armpit.
6. Rest and smile to the tendon line, using your awareness to help absorb chi into the tendon line, replenishing and strengthening it.
7. Repeat on the other side.

Fig. 8.8. The middle toe line

❂ The Middle Toe Line

1. Stand with your left leg a good distance forward, well bent and slightly to the side, but without straining yourself. Hold the mung bean sock in your right hand.
2. Swallow saliva down to your belly and start hitting from the left shoulder.
3. Hit down in a straight line over the left nipple, over the internal organs on the left side of the body, and over the psoas muscle.
4. Cross over to the other side and continue down the right leg, hitting over the top of the thigh muscle, straight over the kneecap (hit beneath the kneecap, not directly on it), all along the outside of the shinbone, over the ankle, and down the middle line of the foot, ending in the middle toe (fig. 8.8).
5. Gently hit the top of the foot, in the middle, an additional 3 times.
6. Follow the same route all the way back up to the shoulder.
7. Rest and smile to the tendon line, using your awareness to help absorb chi into the tendon line, replenishing and strengthening it.
8. Repeat on the other side.

Fig. 8.9. The back of the leg line

☯ The Back of the Leg Line

1. Stand with your left leg a good distance forward, well bent and slightly to the side, but without straining yourself. Hold the mung bean sock in your right hand.
2. Swallow saliva down to your belly and start hitting from the back of the neck.
3. Hit down in a line just to the left of the spine all the way to your tailbone.
4. Continue down the right leg, hitting the back of the thigh muscle, the back of the knee, and all the way down the back of your calf until you reach your heel (fig. 8.9).
5. Follow the same route all the way back up to the neck.
6. Rest and smile to the tendon line, using your awareness to help absorb chi into the tendon line, replenishing and strengthening it.
7. Repeat on the other side.

If consistently practiced, these simple techniques are guaranteed to strengthen the tendons greatly, especially when combined with Tendon Nei Kung practice. Most people end up suffering tremendously from joint problems when they move into old age. This unnecessary suffering can so easily be prevented. Prevention is the best medicine, and though these same exercises can be used to heal tendons after they are injured, it is far more effective to start doing the practices before you begin experiencing problems.

Recommended Practice for Today's Lifestyle

The Tendon Nei Kung forms themselves should constitute the bulk of your tendon-strengthening (growing) practice and should be given most attention (fig. 9.1). Initially it is important to set some time aside to make sure that you are doing the forms correctly, without neglecting any of the details, as people are sometimes inclined to do. Make sure you study the information on doing the forms thoroughly. Do not be in a hurry to reach the point where you can do the complete movements of the forms. These special exercises have many subtle details.

You could probably perfect the outer movements within three days if you have physical aptitude and a strong intent to learn and practice. However, Chi Kung is not called an internal practice for nothing, and mastering all the internal and external aspects of the movements together takes a little perseverance and patience. Once you have the external movements down and can execute them without thinking about it, start paying attention to the internal movements, and try to sense the internal force coming up from the ground all the way into your fingertips. If you practice in this way it will not be long before you can execute the movements correctly, and as the Taoist love to say, "Once you have it, you have it."

Mastering the Tendon Nei Kung forms is well worth your time and energy, as you will receive priceless benefits from practicing them correctly. This practice enables you not only to cultivate great strength but also to save yourself much of the suffering and indignity that people have come to accept as the normal deterioration of old age. The best approach is to build up your Tendon Nei Kung form practice step by step, being sure to master each step before you move on to the next one. Once you have cultivated a level of mastery over the basic structure of the forms in this way, learning the eight different hand positions should not be too much of a challenge.

Fig. 9.1. Tendon Nei Kung practice

Ten repetitions of each hand position is already a substantial tendon-strengthening workout and is a sufficient daily practice. Once you are doing them properly, the hand movements should take you no longer than 10 minutes a day. It is important not to exceed the advised number of repetitions, especially if you are new to these techniques, as straining a tendon is both an unpleasant experience and a potentially chronic injury. In Taoist practices moderation is always the motto, as the Taoists understand the importance of both the practice itself and the resting period, in which the body has a chance to nourish the area that has been given attention. Even Western scientists arc now seeing the benefits of such a rest period. For example, they have discovered that for optimal results in weight lifting, it is essential for the lifter to give a worked-out muscle at least a 48-hour rest before exercising it again. If the lifter does not allow the muscle this recuperation period, the muscle runs a high risk of actually becoming weaker.

If you have a partner at hand and have the time, you may wish to add another ten repetitions of all the hand positions in the partner forms, which should take another 10 minutes. Of course partner practice should be integrated into your practice only once your solo practice is of a high level. The partner forms are also very helpful in determining whether you are doing the movements of the forms correctly.

A session of Mung Bean Hitting should also be done every day, preferably just before you do the Tendon Nei Kung forms, as this practice will aid the tendon-growing process greatly (fig. 9.2). If you are highly motivated to improve the quality and strength of your tendons and have ample time, you can do a very thorough hitting session of 20 to 25 minutes. A more general workout with the mung bean sock will take only about 8 to 10 minutes. This practice is especially helpful in the reparation of damaged tendons and joints and greatly assists the Tendon Nei Kung forms in working their magic.

The supplementary tendon exercises should be practiced a minimum of twice a week. If, however, you have available time, please

Fig. 9.2. Mung Bean Hitting

indulge yourself in doing these every day. Be careful, of course, not to do too much in one day. Combining these three practices will yield optimal results.

Tendons strength is extremely long lasting, as we discussed earlier in this book. However, tendons also take longer than muscles to strengthen. Patience is an essential ingredient in the makeup of someone wishing to pursue tendon-growing practices. As a wise man once said to me, Tai Chi Chi Kung practices are not microwave pizzas. The rewards of your practices are inevitable, but it is important not to become fixated upon results. Concentrating on results is a cause of grief for many people in many areas of their lives. When you are concentrated on a result, it is very difficult to fall into a state of calm and meditation, which is the ultimate state to be in for Chi Kung practice—or whatever you are doing, for that matter (fig. 9. 3). An important component of a meditative state is to be present from moment to moment, and concentrating on results obviously prevents you from doing this. If you practice consistently, though, after a 6-month period you will already start experiencing the fantastic benefits of this practice and will begin to feel a new kind of strength in your body—a genuine strength.

Fig. 9.3. Meditative state

For all of the above-mentioned practices, remember to take the time to shake out, rest, and smile to the tendons that have been given attention. This takes only 20 seconds or so, and it is a vital practice for strengthening tendons and most Chi Kung practices, greatly increasing the benefits of the exercises.

Once again we remind you to stay mentally present during the practice of these exercises. Remember, chi follows Yi, or energy follows mind. The more chi your tendons receive, the more they will be able to effortlessly strengthen. If your mind is on other things, the effect of the Tendon Nei Kung exercises will be greatly subdued.

Finally, we would like to encourage you to adopt a superior tendon-changing attitude. It is important that you do not adopt the stereotypical "body builder" mentality toward tendon workouts, as this will not provide superior results. If you encounter pain in any of these exercises, do not push yourself. Build up all of the practices slowly and gently, leaving any macho "no pain, no gain" attitude at the door, and start to trust in the effortless path of the Tao.

Good luck, and may the chi be with you!

 # About the Author

Mantak Chia has been studying the Taoist approach to life since childhood. His mastery of this ancient knowledge, enhanced by his study of other disciplines, has resulted in the development of the Universal Tao System, which is now being taught throughout the world.

Mantak Chia was born in Thailand to Chinese parents in 1944. When he was six years old, he learned from Buddhist monks how to sit and "still the mind." While in grammar school he learned traditional Thai boxing, and soon he went on to acquire considerable skill in Aikido, Yoga, and Tai Chi. His studies of the Taoist way of life began in earnest when he was a student in Hong Kong, ultimately leading to his mastery of a wide variety of esoteric disciplines, with the guidance of several masters, including Master I Yun, Master Meugi, Master Cheng Yao Lun, and Master Pan Yu. To better understand the mechanisms behind healing energy, he also studied Western anatomy and medical sciences.

Master Chia has taught his system of healing and energizing practices to tens of thousands of students and has trained more than two thousand instructors and practitioners throughout the world. He has established centers for Taoist study and training in many countries around the globe. In June 1990 he was honored by the International Congress of Chinese Medicine and Qi Gong (Chi Kung), which named him the Qi Gong Master of the Year.

The Universal Tao System and Training Center

THE UNIVERSAL TAO SYSTEM

The ultimate goal of Taoist practice is to transcend physical boundaries through the development of the soul and the spirit within the human. That is also the guiding principle behind the Universal Tao, a practical system of self-development that enables individuals to complete the harmonious evolution of their physical, mental, and spiritual bodies. Through a series of ancient Chinese meditative and internal energy exercises, the practitioner learns to increase physical energy, release tension, improve health, practice self-defense, and gain the ability to heal him- or herself and others. In the process of creating a solid foundation of health and well-being in the physical body, the practitioner also creates the basis for developing his or her spiritual potential by learning to tap into the natural energies of the sun, moon, earth, stars, and other environmental forces.

The Universal Tao practices are derived from ancient techniques rooted in the processes of nature. They have been gathered and integrated into a coherent, accessible system for well-being that works directly with the life force, or chi, that flows through the meridian system of the body.

Master Chia has spent years developing and perfecting techniques for teaching these traditional practices to students around the world through ongoing classes, workshops, private instruction, and healing sessions, as well as books and video and audio products. Further information can be obtained at www.universal-tao.com.

THE UNIVERSAL TAO TRAINING CENTER

The Tao Garden Resort and Training Center in northern Thailand is the home of Master Chia and serves as the worldwide headquarters for Universal Tao activities. This integrated wellness, holistic health, and training center is situated on eighty acres surrounded by the beautiful Himalayan foothills near the historic walled city of Chiang Mai. The serene setting includes flower and herb gardens ideal for meditation, open-air pavilions for practicing Chi Kung, and a health and fitness spa.

The center offers classes year-round, as well as summer and winter retreats. It can accommodate two hundred students, and group leasing can be arranged. For information worldwide on courses, books, products, and other resources, see below.

RESOURCES

Universal Healing Tao Center
274 Moo 7, Luang Nua, Doi Saket, Chiang Mai, 50220 Thailand
Tel: (66)(53) 495-596 Fax: (66)(53) 495-852
E-mail: universaltao@universal-tao.com
Web site: www.universal-tao.com

For information on retreats and the health spa, contact:
Tao Garden Health Spa & Resort
E-mail: info@tao-garden.com, taogarden@hotmail.com
Web site: www.tao-garden.com

Good Chi • Good Heart • Good Intention

Index

Pages in *italic* refer to illustrations.

BOOKS OF RELATED INTEREST

Inner Traditions • Bear & Company
P.O. Box 388
Rochester, VT 05767
1-800-246-8648
www.InnerTraditions.com

Or contact your local bookseller